the WAR of ART

ALSO BY STEVEN PRESSFIELD

FICTION

The Profession

Killing Rommel

The Afghan Campaign

The Virtues of War

Last of the Amazons

Tides of War

Gates of Fire

The Legend of Bagger Vance

NONFICTION

Turning Pro

Do the Work

The Warrior Ethos

the WAR of ART

Break Through the Blocks
and Win Your
Inner Creative Battles

STEVEN PRESSFIELD

Black Irish Entertainment LLC

NEW YORK   LOS ANGELES

BLACK IRISH ENTERTAINMENT LLC

65 CENTRAL PARK WEST

NEW YORK, NY 10023

COPYRIGHT © 2002 BY STEVEN PRESSFIELD

COVER DESIGN BY BRIGID PEARSON

COVER ILLUSTRATION BY MILTON GLASER

FIRST BLACK IRISH ENTERTAINMENT PAPERBACK EDITION JANUARY 2012

FOR INFORMATION ABOUT SPECIAL DISCOUNTS FOR BULK PURCHASES,

PLEASE VISIT WWW.STEVENPRESSFIELD.COM OR WWW.BLACKIRISHBOOKS.COM

ISBN: 978-1-936891-02-3

THE LIBRARY OF CONGRESS HAS CATALOGUED

THE HARDCOVER EDITION AS FOLLOWS:

Pressfield, Steven.

The war of art : winning the inner creative battle / Steven Pressfield;

forward by Robert McKee. —1st ed.

P. CM.

ISBN: 1-59071-003-7

1. Creative ability. 2. Creative thinking. 3. Authorship. I. Title.

BF408.P74 2002 153.3'5

QB102-701260

PRINTED IN THE UNITED STATES OF AMERICA

1   2   3   4   5   6   7   8   9   10

for

BERNAY

FOREWORD

by Robert McKee

Steven Pressfield wrote *The War of Art* for me. He undoubtedly wrote it for you too, but I know he did it expressly for me because I hold Olympic records for procrastination. I can procrastinate thinking about my procrastination problem. I can procrastinate dealing with my problem of procrastinating thinking about my procrastination problem. So Pressfield, that devil, asked me to write this foreword *against a deadline,* knowing that no matter how much I stalled, eventually I'd have to knuckle down and do the work. At the last possible hour I did, and as I leafed through Book One, "Defining the Enemy," I saw myself staring back guilty-eyed from every page. But then Book Two gave me a battle plan; Book Three, a vision of victory; and as I closed *The War of Art,* I felt a surge of positive calm. I now know I can win this war. And if I can, so can you.

To begin Book One, Pressfield labels the enemy of creativity Resistance, his all-encompassing term for what Freud called the Death Wish—that destructive force inside human nature that rises whenever we consider a tough, long-term course of action that might do for us or others something that's actually good. He then presents a rogue's gallery of the many manifestations of Resistance. You will recognize each and every one, for this force lives within us all—self-sabotage, self-deception, self-corruption. We writers know it as "block," a paralysis whose symptoms can bring on appalling behavior.

Some years ago I was as blocked as a Calcutta sewer, so what did I do? I decided to try on all my clothes. To show just how anal I can get, I put on every shirt, pair of pants, sweater, jacket, and sock, sorting them into piles: spring, summer, fall, winter, Salvation Army. Then I tried them on all over again, this time parsing them into spring casual, spring formal, summer casual . . . Two days of this and I thought I was going mad. Want to know how to cure writer's block? It's not a trip to your psychiatrist. For as Pressfield wisely points out, seeking "support" is Resistance at its most seductive. No, the cure is found in Book Two: "Turning Pro."

Steven Pressfield is the very definition of a pro. I know this because I can't count the times I called the author of *The Legend of Bagger Vance* to invite him for a round of golf, and although tempted, he declined. Why? Because he was working, and as any writer who has ever taken a backswing knows, golf is a beautifully virulent form of procrastination. In other words, Resistance. Steve packs a discipline forged of Bethlehem steel.

I read Steve's *Gates of Fire* and *Tides of War* back-to-back while traveling in Europe. Now, I'm not a lachrymose guy; I hadn't cried over a book since *The Red Pony,* but these novels got to me. I found myself sitting in cafés, choking back tears over the selfless courage of those Greeks who shaped and saved Western civilization. As I looked beneath his seamless prose and sensed his depth of research, of knowledge of human nature and society, of vividly imagined telling details, I was in awe of the work, the work, all the work that built the foundation of his riveting creations. And I'm not alone in this appreciation. When I bought the books in London, I was told that Steve's novels are now assigned by Oxford history dons who tell their students that if they wish to rub shoulders with life in classical Greece, read Pressfield.

How does an artist achieve that power? In the second book Pressfield lays out the day-by-day, step-by-step campaign of the professional: preparation, order, patience, endurance, acting in the face of fear and failure—no excuses, no bullshit. And best of all, Steve's brilliant insight that first, last, and always, the professional focuses on mastery of the craft.

Book Three, "The Higher Realm," looks at Inspiration, that sublime result that blossoms in the furrows of the professional who straps on the harness and plows the fields of his or her art. In Pressfield's words: "When we sit down each day and do our work, power concentrates around us... we become like a magnetized rod that attracts iron filings. Ideas come. Insights accrete." On this, the *effect* of Inspiration, Steve and I absolutely agree. Indeed, stunning images and ideas arrive as if from nowhere. In fact, these seemingly spontaneous flashes are so amazing, it's hard to believe that our unworthy selves created them. From where, therefore, does our best stuff come?

It's on this point, however, the *cause* of Inspiration, that we see things differently. In Book One Steve traces Resistance down its evolutionary roots to the genes. I agree. The cause is genetic. That negative force, that dark antagonism to creativity, is embedded deep in our humanity. But in Book Three he shifts gears and looks for the cause of Inspiration not in human nature, but on a "higher realm." Then with a poetic fire he lays out his belief in muses and angels. The ultimate source of creativity, he argues, is divine. Many, perhaps most readers, will find Book Three profoundly moving.

I, on the other hand, believe that the source of creativity is found on the same plane of reality as Resistance. It, too, is genetic. It's called talent: the innate power to discover the hidden connection between two things—images, ideas, words—that no one else has ever seen before, link them, and create for the world a third, utterly unique work. Like our IQ, talent is a gift from our ancestors. If we're lucky, we inherit it. In the fortunate talented few, the dark dimension of their natures will first resist the labor that creativity demands, but once they commit to the task, their talented side stirs to action and rewards them with astonishing feats. These flashes of creative genius seem to arrive from out of the blue for the obvious reason: They come from the unconscious mind. In short, if the Muse exists, she does not whisper to the untalented.

So although Steve and I may differ on the cause, we agree on the effect: When inspiration touches talent, she gives birth to truth and beauty. And when Steven Pressfield was writing *The War of Art*, she had her hands all over him.

THE WAR OF ART

WHAT I DO

I get up, take a shower, have breakfast. I read the paper, brush my teeth. If I have phone calls to make, I make them. I've got my coffee now. I put on my lucky work boots and stitch up the lucky laces that my niece Meredith gave me. I head back to my office, crank up the computer. My lucky hooded sweatshirt is draped over the chair, with the lucky charm I got from a gypsy in Saintes-Maries-de-la-Mer for only eight bucks in francs, and my lucky LARGO nametag that came from a dream I once had. I put it on. On my thesaurus is my lucky cannon that my friend Bob Versandi gave me from Morro Castle, Cuba. I point it toward my chair, so it can fire inspiration into me. I say my prayer, which is the Invocation of the Muse from Homer's *Odyssey*, translation by T. E. Lawrence, Lawrence of Arabia, which my dear mate Paul Rink gave me and which sits near my shelf with the cuff links that belonged to my father and my lucky acorn from the battlefield at Thermopylae. It's about ten-thirty now. I sit down and plunge in. When I start making typos, I know I'm getting tired. That's four hours or so. I've hit the point of diminishing returns. I wrap for the day. Copy whatever I've done to disk and stash the disk in the glove compartment of my truck in case there's a fire and I have to run for it. I power down. It's three, three-thirty. The office is closed. How many pages have I produced? I don't care. Are they any good? I don't even think about it. All that matters is I've put in my time and hit it with all I've got. All that counts is that, for this day, for this session, I have overcome Resistance.

WHAT I KNOW

There's a secret that real writers know that wannabe writers don't, and the secret is this: It's not the writing part that's hard. What's hard is sitting down to write. What keeps us from sitting down is Resistance.

THE UNLIVED LIFE

Most of us have two lives. The life we live, and the unlived life within us. Between the two stands Resistance.

Have you ever brought home a treadmill and let it gather dust in the attic? Ever quit a diet, a course of yoga, a meditation practice? Have you ever bailed out on a call to embark upon a spiritual practice, dedicate yourself to a humanitarian calling, commit your life to the service of others? Have you ever wanted to be a mother, a doctor, an advocate for the weak and helpless; to run for office, crusade for the planet, campaign for world peace, or to preserve the environment? Late at night have you experienced a vision of the person you might become, the work you could accomplish, the realized being you were meant to be? Are you a writer who doesn't write, a painter who doesn't paint, an entrepreneur who never starts a venture? Then you know what Resistance is.

> One night I was layin' down,
> I heard Papa talkin' to Mama.
> I heard Papa say, to let that boy boogie-woogie.
> 'Cause it's in him and it's got to come out.
> —John Lee Hooker, "Boogie Chillen"

Resistance is the most toxic force on the planet. It is the root of more unhappiness than poverty, disease, and erectile dysfunction. To yield to Resistance deforms our spirit. It stunts us and makes us less than we are and were born to be. If you believe in God (and I do) you must declare Resistance evil, for it prevents us from achieving the life God intended when He endowed each of us with our own unique genius. *Genius* is a Latin word; the Romans used it to denote an inner spirit, holy and inviolable, which watches over us, guiding us to our calling. A writer writes with his *genius;* an artist paints with hers; everyone who creates operates from this sacramental center. It is our soul's seat, the vessel that holds our being-in-potential, our star's beacon and Polaris.

Every sun casts a shadow, and genius's shadow is Resistance. As powerful as is our soul's call to realization, so potent are the forces of Resistance arrayed against it. Resistance is faster than a speeding bullet, more powerful than a locomotive, harder to kick than crack cocaine. We're not alone if we've been mowed down by Resistance; millions of good men and women have bitten the dust before us. And here's the biggest bitch: We don't even know what hit us. I never did. From age twenty-four to thirty-two, Resistance kicked my ass from East Coast to West and back again thirteen times and I never even knew it existed. I looked everywhere for the enemy and failed to see it right in front of my face.

Have you heard this story: Woman learns she has cancer, six months to live. Within days she quits her job, resumes the dream of writing Tex-Mex songs she gave up to raise a family (or starts studying classical Greek, or moves to the inner city and devotes herself to tending babies with AIDS). Woman's friends think she's crazy; she herself has never been happier. There's a postscript. Woman's cancer goes into remission.

Is that what it takes? Do we have to stare death in the face to make us stand up and confront Resistance? Does Resistance have to cripple and disfigure our lives before we wake up to its existence? How many of us have become drunks and drug addicts, developed tumors and neuroses, succumbed to painkillers, gossip, and compulsive cell-phone use, simply because we don't do that thing that our hearts, our inner genius, is calling us to? Resistance defeats us. If tomorrow morning by some stroke of magic every dazed and benighted soul woke up with the power to take the first step toward pursuing his or her dreams, every shrink in the directory would be out of business. Prisons would stand empty. The alcohol and tobacco industries would collapse, along with the junk food, cosmetic surgery, and infotainment businesses, not to mention pharmaceutical companies, hospitals, and the medical profession from top to bottom. Domestic abuse would become extinct, as would addiction, obesity, migraine headaches, road rage, and dandruff.

Look in your own heart. Unless I'm crazy, right now a still small voice is piping up, telling you as it has ten thousand times, the calling that is yours and yours alone. You know it. No one has to tell you. And unless I'm crazy, you're no closer to taking action on it than you were yesterday or will be tomorrow. You think Resistance isn't real? Resistance will bury you.

You know, Hitler wanted to be an artist. At eighteen he took his inheritance, seven hundred kronen, and moved to Vienna to live and study. He applied to the Academy of Fine Arts and later to the School of Architecture. Ever see one of his paintings? Neither have I. Resistance beat him. Call it overstatement but I'll say it anyway: it was easier for Hitler to start World War II than it was for him to face a blank square of canvas.

BOOK ONE

RESISTANCE

Defining the Enemy

The enemy is a very good teacher.

—the Dalai Lama

RESISTANCE'S GREATEST HITS

The following is a list, in no particular order, of those activities that most commonly elicit Resistance:

1) The pursuit of any calling in writing, painting, music, film, dance, or any creative art, however marginal or unconventional.

2) The launching of any entrepreneurial venture or enterprise, for profit or otherwise.

3) Any diet or health regimen.

4) Any program of spiritual advancement.

5) Any activity whose aim is tighter abdominals.

6) Any course or program designed to overcome an unwholesome habit or addiction.

7) Education of every kind.

8) Any act of political, moral, or ethical courage, including the decision to change for the better some unworthy pattern of thought or conduct in ourselves.

9) The undertaking of any enterprise or endeavor whose aim is to help others.

10) Any act that entails commitment of the heart. The decision to get married, to have a child, to weather a rocky patch in a relationship.

11) The taking of any principled stand in the face of adversity.

In other words, any act that rejects immediate gratification in favor of long-term growth, health, or integrity. Or, expressed another way, any act that derives from our higher nature instead of our lower. Any of these will elicit Resistance.

Now: what are the characteristics of Resistance?

RESISTANCE IS INVISIBLE

Resistance cannot be seen, touched, heard, or smelled. But it can be felt. We experience it as an energy field radiating from a work-in-potential. It's a repelling force. It's negative. Its aim is to shove us away, distract us, prevent us from doing our work.

RESISTANCE IS INTERNAL

Resistance seems to come from outside ourselves. We locate it in spouses, jobs, bosses, kids. "Peripheral opponents," as Pat Riley used to say when he coached the Los Angeles Lakers.

Resistance is not a peripheral opponent. Resistance arises from within. It is self-generated and self-perpetuated. Resistance is the enemy within.

RESISTANCE IS INSIDIOUS

Resistance will tell you anything to keep you from doing your work. It will perjure, fabricate, falsify; seduce, bully, cajole. Resistance is protean. It will assume any form, if that's what it takes to deceive you. It will reason with you like a lawyer or jam a nine-millimeter in your face like a stickup man. Resistance has no conscience. It will pledge anything to get a deal, then double-cross you as soon as your back is turned. If you take Resistance at its word, you deserve everything you get. Resistance is always lying and always full of shit.

RESISTANCE IS IMPLACABLE

Resistance is like the Alien or the Terminator or the shark in *Jaws*. It cannot be reasoned with. It understands nothing but power. It is an engine of destruction, programmed from the factory with one object only: to prevent us from doing our work. Resistance is implacable, intractable, indefatigable. Reduce it to a single cell and that cell will continue to attack.

This is Resistance's nature. It's all it knows.

RESISTANCE IS IMPERSONAL

Resistance is not out to get you personally. It doesn't know who you are and doesn't care. Resistance is a force of nature. It acts objectively.

Though it feels malevolent, Resistance in fact operates with the indifference of rain and transits the heavens by the same laws as the stars. When we marshal our forces to combat Resistance, we must remember this.

RESISTANCE IS INFALLIBLE

L ike a magnetized needle floating on a surface of oil, Resistance will unfailingly point to true North—meaning that calling or action it most wants to stop us from doing.

We can use this. We can use it as a compass. We can navigate by Resistance, letting it guide us to that calling or action that we must follow before all others.

Rule of thumb: The more important a call or action is to our soul's evolution, the more Resistance we will feel toward pursuing it.

RESISTANCE IS UNIVERSAL

We're wrong if we think we're the only ones struggling with Resistance. Everyone who has a body experiences Resistance.

RESISTANCE NEVER SLEEPS

Henry Fonda was still throwing up before each stage performance, even when he was seventy-five. In other words, fear doesn't go away. The warrior and the artist live by the same code of necessity, which dictates that the battle must be fought anew every day.

RESISTANCE PLAYS FOR KEEPS

Resistance's goal is not to wound or disable. Resistance aims to kill. Its target is the epicenter of our being: our genius, our soul, the unique and priceless gift we were put on earth to give and that no one else has but us. Resistance means business. When we fight it, we are in a war to the death.

RESISTANCE IS FUELED BY FEAR

Resistance has no strength of its own. Every ounce of juice it possesses comes from us. We feed it with power by our fear of it.

Master that fear and we conquer Resistance.

RESISTANCE ONLY OPPOSES
IN ONE DIRECTION

Resistance obstructs movement only from a lower sphere to a higher. It kicks in when we seek to pursue a calling in the arts, launch an innovative enterprise, or evolve to a higher station morally, ethically, or spiritually.

So if you're in Calcutta working with the Mother Teresa Foundation and you're thinking of bolting to launch a career in telemarketing. . . relax. Resistance will give you a free pass.

RESISTANCE IS MOST POWERFUL
AT THE FINISH LINE

Odysseus almost got home years before his actual homecoming. Ithaca was in sight, close enough that the sailors could see the smoke of their families' fires on shore. Odysseus was so certain he was safe, he actually lay down for a snooze. It was then that his men, believing there was gold in an ox-hide sack among their commander's possessions, snatched this prize and cut it open. The bag contained the adverse Winds, which King Aeolus had bottled up for Odysseus when the wanderer had touched earlier at his blessed isle. The winds burst forth now in one mad blow, driving Odysseus' ships back across every league of ocean they had with such difficulty traversed, making him endure further trials and sufferings before, at last and alone, he reached home for good.

The danger is greatest when the finish line is in sight. At this point, Resistance knows we're about to beat it. It hits the panic button. It marshals one last assault and slams us with everything it's got.

The professional must be alert for this counterattack. Be wary at the end. Don't open that bag of wind.

RESISTANCE RECRUITS ALLIES

Resistance by definition is self-sabotage. But there's a parallel peril that must also be guarded against: sabotage by others.

When a writer begins to overcome her Resistance—in other words, when she actually starts to write—she may find that those close to her begin acting strange. They may become moody or sullen, they may get sick; they may accuse the awakening writer of "changing," of "not being the person she was." The closer these people are to the awakening writer, the more bizarrely they will act and the more emotion they will put behind their actions.

They are trying to sabotage her.

The reason is that they are struggling, consciously or unconsciously, against their own Resistance. The awakening writer's success becomes a reproach to them. If she can beat these demons, why can't they?

Often couples or close friends, even entire families, will enter into tacit compacts whereby each individual pledges (unconsciously) to remain mired in the same slough in which she and all her cronies have become so comfortable. The highest treason a crab can commit is to make a leap for the rim of the bucket.

The awakening artist must be ruthless, not only with herself but with others. Once you make your break, you can't turn around for your buddy who catches his trouser leg on the barbed wire. The best thing you can do for that friend (and he'd tell you this himself, if he really is your friend) is to get over the wall and keep motating.

The best and only thing that one artist can do for another is to serve as an example and an inspiration.

Now, let's consider the next aspect of Resistance: symptoms.

RESISTANCE AND PROCRASTINATION

Procrastination is the most common manifestation of Resistance because it's the easiest to rationalize. We don't tell ourselves, "I'm never going to write my symphony." Instead we say, "I am going to write my symphony; I'm just going to start tomorrow."

RESISTANCE AND PROCRASTINATION,
PART TWO

The most pernicious aspect of procrastination is that it can become a habit. We don't just put off our lives today; we put them off till our deathbed.

Never forget: This very moment, we can change our lives. There never was a moment, and never will be, when we are without the power to alter our destiny. This second, we can turn the tables on Resistance.

This second, we can sit down and do our work.

RESISTANCE AND SEX

S ometimes Resistance takes the form of sex, or an obsessive preoccupation with sex. Why sex? Because sex provides immediate and powerful gratification. When someone sleeps with us, we feel validated and approved of, even loved. Resistance gets a big kick out of that. It knows it has distracted us with a cheap, easy fix and kept us from doing our work.

Of course not all sex is a manifestation of Resistance. In my experience, you can tell by the measure of hollowness you feel afterward. The more empty you feel, the more certain you can be that your true motivation was not love or even lust but Resistance.

It goes without saying that this principle applies to drugs, shopping, masturbation, TV, gossip, alcohol, and the consumption of all products containing fat, sugar, salt, or chocolate.

RESISTANCE AND TROUBLE

We get ourselves in trouble because it's a cheap way to get attention. Trouble is a faux form of fame. It's easier to get busted in the bedroom with the faculty chairman's wife than it is to finish that dissertation on the metaphysics of motley in the novellas of Joseph Conrad.

Ill health is a form of trouble, as are alcoholism and drug addiction, proneness to accidents, all neurosis including compulsive screwing-up, and such seemingly benign foibles as jealousy, chronic lateness, and the blasting of rap music at 110 dB from your smoked-glass '95 Supra. Anything that draws attention to ourselves through pain-free or artificial means is a manifestation of Resistance.

Cruelty to others is a form of Resistance, as is the willing endurance of cruelty from others.

The working artist will not tolerate trouble in her life because she knows trouble prevents her from doing her work. The working artist banishes from her world all sources of trouble. She harnesses the urge for trouble and transforms it in her work.

RESISTANCE AND SELF-DRAMATIZATION

Creating soap opera in our lives is a symptom of Resistance. Why put in years of work designing a new software interface when you can get just as much attention by bringing home a boyfriend with a prison record?

Sometimes entire families participate unconsciously in a culture of self-dramatization. The kids fuel the tanks, the grown-ups arm the phasers, the whole starship lurches from one spine-tingling episode to another. And the crew knows how to keep it going. If the level of drama drops below a certain threshold, someone jumps in to amp it up. Dad gets drunk, Mom gets sick, Janie shows up for church with an Oakland Raiders tattoo. It's more fun than a movie. And it works: Nobody gets a damn thing done.

Sometimes I think of Resistance as a sort of evil twin to Santa Claus, who makes his rounds house-to-house, making sure that everything's taken care of. When he comes to a house that's hooked on self-dramatization, his ruddy cheeks glow and he giddy-ups away behind his eight tiny reindeer. He knows there'll be no work done in that house.

RESISTANCE AND SELF-MEDICATION

D o you regularly ingest any substance, controlled or otherwise, whose aim is the alleviation of depression, anxiety, etc.? I offer the following experience:

I once worked as a writer for a big New York ad agency. Our boss used to tell us: Invent a disease. Come up with the disease, he said, and we can sell the cure.

Attention Deficit Disorder, Seasonal Affect Disorder, Social Anxiety Disorder. These aren't diseases, they're marketing ploys. Doctors didn't discover them, copywriters did. Marketing departments did. Drug companies did.

Depression and anxiety may be real. But they can also be Resistance.

When we drug ourselves to blot out our soul's call, we are being good Americans and exemplary consumers. We're doing exactly what TV commercials and pop materialist culture have been brainwashing us to do from birth. Instead of applying self-knowledge, self-discipline, delayed gratification, and hard work, we simply consume a product.

Many pedestrians have been maimed or killed at the intersection of Resistance and Commerce.

RESISTANCE AND VICTIMHOOD

D octors estimate that seventy to eighty percent of their business is non–health-related. People aren't sick, they're self-dramatizing. Sometimes the hardest part of a medical job is keeping a straight face. As Jerry Seinfeld observed of his twenty years of dating: "That's a lot of acting fascinated."

The acquisition of a condition lends significance to one's existence. An illness, a cross to bear. . . Some people go from condition to condition; they cure one, and another pops up to take its place. The condition becomes a work of art in itself, a shadow version of the real creative act the victim is avoiding by expending so much care cultivating his condition.

A victim act is a form of passive aggression. It seeks to achieve gratification not by honest work or a contribution made out of one's experience or insight or love, but by the manipulation of others through silent (and not-so-silent) threat. The victim compels others to come to his rescue or to behave as he wishes by holding them hostage to the prospect of his own further illness/meltdown/mental dissolution, or simply by threatening to make their lives so miserable that they do what he wants.

Casting yourself as a victim is the antithesis of doing your work. Don't do it. If you're doing it, stop.

RESISTANCE AND
THE CHOICE OF A MATE

Sometimes, if we're not conscious of our own Resistance, we'll pick as a mate someone who has or is successfully overcoming Resistance. I'm not sure why. Maybe it's easier to endow our partner with the power that we in fact possess but are afraid to act upon. Maybe it's less threatening to believe that our beloved spouse is worthy to live out his or her unlived life, while we are not. Or maybe we're hoping to use our mate as a model. Maybe we believe (or wish we could) that some of our spouse's power will rub off on us, if we just hang around it long enough.

This is how Resistance disfigures love. The stew it creates is rich, it's colorful; Tennessee Williams could work it up into a trilogy. But is it love? If we're the supporting partner, shouldn't we face our own failure to pursue our unlived life, rather than hitchhike on our spouse's coattails? And if we're the supported partner, shouldn't we step out from the glow of our loved one's adoration and instead encourage him to let his own light shine?

RESISTANCE AND THIS BOOK

When I began this book, Resistance almost beat me. This is the form it took. It told me (the voice in my head) that I was a writer of fiction, not nonfiction, and that I shouldn't be exposing these concepts of Resistance literally and overtly; rather, I should incorporate them metaphorically into a novel. That's a pretty damn subtle and convincing argument. The rationalization Resistance presented me with was that I should write, say, a war piece in which the principles of Resistance were expressed as the fear a warrior feels.

Resistance also told me I shouldn't seek to instruct, or put myself forward as a purveyor of wisdom; that this was vain, egotistical, possibly even corrupt, and that it would work harm to me in the end. That scared me. It made a lot of sense.

What finally convinced me to go ahead was simply that I was so unhappy not going ahead. I was developing symptoms. As soon as I sat down and began, I was okay.

RESISTANCE AND UNHAPPINESS

What does Resistance feel like?

First, unhappiness. We feel like hell. A low-grade misery pervades everything. We're bored, we're restless. We can't get no satisfaction. There's guilt but we can't put our finger on the source. We want to go back to bed; we want to get up and party. We feel unloved and unlovable. We're disgusted. We hate our lives. We hate ourselves.

Unalleviated, Resistance mounts to a pitch that becomes unendurable. At this point vices kick in. Dope, adultery, web surfing.

Beyond that, Resistance becomes clinical. Depression, aggression, dysfunction. Then actual crime and physical self-destruction.

Sounds like life, I know. It isn't. It's Resistance.

What makes it tricky is that we live in a consumer culture that's acutely aware of this unhappiness and has massed all its profit-seeking artillery to exploit it. By selling us a product, a drug, a distraction. John Lennon once wrote:

Well, you think you're so clever
and classless and free
But you're all fucking peasants
As far as I can see

As artists and professionals it is our obligation to enact our own internal revolution, a private insurrection inside our own skulls. In this uprising we free ourselves from the tyranny of consumer culture. We overthrow the programming of advertising, movies, video games, magazines, TV, and MTV by which we have been hypnotized from the cradle. We unplug ourselves from the grid by recognizing that we will never cure our restlessness by contributing our disposable income to the bottom line of Bullshit, Inc., but only by doing our work.

RESISTANCE AND FUNDAMENTALISM

The artist and the fundamentalist both confront the same issue, the mystery of their existence as individuals. Each asks the same questions: Who am I? Why am I here? What is the meaning of my life?

At more primitive stages of evolution, humanity didn't have to deal with such questions. In the states of savagery, of barbarism, in nomadic culture, medieval society, in the tribe and the clan, one's position was fixed by the commandments of the community. It was only with the advent of modernity (starting with the ancient Greeks), with the birth of freedom and of the individual, that such matters ascended to the fore.

These are not easy questions. Who am I? Why am I here? They're not easy because the human being isn't wired to function as an individual. We're wired tribally, to act as part of a group. Our psyches are programmed by millions of years of hunter-gatherer evolution. We know what the clan is; we know how to fit into the band and the tribe. What we don't know is how to be alone. We don't know how to be free individuals.

The artist and the fundamentalist arise from societies at differing stages of development. The artist is the advanced model. His culture possesses affluence, stability, enough excess of resource to permit the luxury of self-examination. The artist is grounded in freedom. He is not afraid of it. He is lucky. He was born in the right place. He has a core of self-confidence, of hope for the future. He believes in progress and evolution. His faith is that humankind is advancing, however haltingly and imperfectly, toward a better world.

The fundamentalist entertains no such notion. In his view, humanity has fallen from a higher state. The truth is not out there awaiting revelation; it has already been revealed. The word of God has been spoken and recorded by His prophet, be he Jesus, Muhammad, or Karl Marx.

Fundamentalism is the philosophy of the powerless, the conquered, the displaced and the dispossessed. Its spawning ground is the wreckage of political and military defeat, as Hebrew fundamentalism arose during the Babylonian captivity, as white Christian fundamentalism appeared in the American South during Reconstruction, as the notion of the Master Race evolved in Germany following World War I. In such desperate times, the vanquished race would perish without a doctrine that restored hope and pride. Islamic fundamentalism ascends from the same landscape of despair and possesses the same tremendous and potent appeal.

What exactly is this despair? It is the despair of freedom. The dislocation and emasculation experienced by the individual cut free from the familiar and comforting structures of the tribe and the clan, the village and the family.

It is the state of modern life.

The fundamentalist (or, more accurately, the beleaguered individual who comes to embrace fundamentalism) cannot stand freedom. He cannot find his way into the future, so he retreats to the past. He returns in imagination to the glory days of his race and seeks to reconstitute both them and himself in their purer, more virtuous light. He gets back to basics. To fundamentals.

Fundamentalism and art are mutually exclusive. There is no such thing as fundamentalist art. This does not mean that the fundamentalist is not creative. Rather, his creativity is inverted. He creates destruction. Even the structures he builds, his schools and networks of organization, are dedicated to annihilation, of his enemies and of himself.

But the fundamentalist reserves his greatest creativity for the fashioning of Satan, the image of his foe, in opposition to which he defines and gives meaning to his own life. Like the artist, the fundamentalist experiences Resistance. He experiences it as temptation to sin. Resistance to the fundamentalist is the call of the Evil One, seeking to seduce him from his virtue. The fundamentalist is consumed with Satan, whom he loves as he loves death. Is it coincidence that the suicide bombers of the World Trade Center frequented strip clubs during their training, or that they conceived of their reward as a squadron of virgin brides and the license to ravish them in the fleshpots of heaven? The fundamentalist hates and fears women because he sees them as vessels of Satan, temptresses like Delilah who seduced Samson from his power.

To combat the call of sin, i.e., Resistance, the fundamentalist plunges either into action or into the study of sacred texts. He loses himself in these, much as the artist does in the process of creation. The difference is that while the one looks forward, hoping to create a better world, the other looks backward, seeking to return to a purer world from which he and all have fallen.

The humanist believes that humankind, as individuals, is called upon to co-create the world with God. This is why he values human life so highly. In his view, things do progress, life does evolve; each individual has value, at least potentially, in advancing this cause. The fundamentalist cannot conceive of this. In his society, dissent is not just crime but apostasy; it is heresy, transgression against God Himself.

When fundamentalism wins, the world enters a dark age. Yet still I can't condemn one who is drawn to this philosophy. I consider my own inner journey, the advantages I've had of education, affluence, family support, health, and the blind good luck to be born American, and still I have learned to exist as an autonomous individual, if indeed I have, only by a whisker, and at a cost I would hate to have to reckon up.

It may be that the human race is not ready for freedom. The air of liberty may be too rarefied for us to breathe. Certainly I wouldn't be writing this book, on this subject, if living with freedom were easy. The paradox seems to be, as Socrates demonstrated long ago, that the truly free individual is free only to the extent of his own self-mastery. While those who will not govern themselves are condemned to find masters to govern over them.

RESISTANCE AND CRITICISM

I f you find yourself criticizing other people, you're probably doing it out of Resistance. When we see others beginning to live their authentic selves, it drives us crazy if we have not lived out our own.

Individuals who are realized in their own lives almost never criticize others. If they speak at all, it is to offer encouragement. Watch yourself. Of all the manifestations of Resistance, most only harm ourselves. Criticism and cruelty harm others as well.

RESISTANCE AND SELF-DOUBT

Self-doubt can be an ally. This is because it serves as an indicator of aspiration. It reflects love, love of something we dream of doing, and desire, desire to do it. If you find yourself asking yourself (and your friends), "Am I really a writer? Am I really an artist?" chances are you are.

The counterfeit innovator is wildly self-confident. The real one is scared to death.

RESISTANCE AND FEAR

A re you paralyzed with fear? That's a good sign.

Fear is good. Like self-doubt, fear is an indicator. Fear tells us what we have to do.

Remember our rule of thumb: The more scared we are of a work or calling, the more sure we can be that we have to do it.

Resistance is experienced as fear; the degree of fear equates to the strength of Resistance. Therefore the more fear we feel about a specific enterprise, the more certain we can be that that enterprise is important to us and to the growth of our soul. That's why we feel so much Resistance. If it meant nothing to us, there'd be no Resistance.

Have you ever watched *Inside the Actors Studio?* The host, James Lipton, invariably asks his guests, "What factors make you decide to take a particular role?" The actor always answers: "Because I'm afraid of it."

The professional tackles the project that will make him stretch. He takes on the assignment that will bear him into uncharted waters, compel him to explore unconscious parts of himself.

Is he scared? Hell, yes. He's petrified.

(Conversely, the professional turns down roles that he's done before. He's not afraid of them anymore. Why waste his time?)

So if you're paralyzed with fear, it's a good sign. It shows you what you have to do.

RESISTANCE AND LOVE

Resistance is directly proportional to love. If you're feeling massive Resistance, the good news is, it means there's tremendous love there too. If you didn't love the project that is terrifying you, you wouldn't feel anything. The opposite of love isn't hate; it's indifference.

The more Resistance you experience, the more important your unmanifested art/project/enterprise is to you—and the more gratification you will feel when you finally do it.

RESISTANCE AND BEING A STAR

G randiose fantasies are a symptom of Resistance. They're the sign of an amateur. The professional has learned that success, like happiness, comes as a by-product of work. The professional concentrates on the work and allows rewards to come or not come, whatever they like.

RESISTANCE AND ISOLATION

S ometimes we balk at embarking on an enterprise because we're afraid of being alone. We feel comfortable with the tribe around us; it makes us nervous going off into the woods on our own.

Here's the trick: We're never alone. As soon as we step outside the campfire glow, our Muse lights on our shoulder like a butterfly. The act of courage calls forth infallibly that deeper part of ourselves that supports and sustains us.

Have you seen interviews with the young John Lennon or Bob Dylan, when the reporter tries to ask about their personal selves? The boys deflect these queries with withering sarcasm. Why? Because Lennon and Dylan know that the part of them that writes the songs is not "them," not the personal self that is of such surpassing fascination to their boneheaded interrogators. Lennon and Dylan also know that the part of themselves that does the writing is too sacred, too precious, too fragile to be redacted into sound bites for the titillation of would-be idolators (who are themselves caught up in their own Resistance). So they put them on and blow them off.

It is a commonplace among artists and children at play that

they're not aware of time or solitude while they're chasing their vision. The hours fly. The sculptress and the tree-climbing tyke both look up blinking when Mom calls, "Suppertime!"

RESISTANCE AND ISOLATION,
PART TWO

Friends sometimes ask, "Don't you get lonely sitting by yourself all day?" At first it seemed odd to hear myself answer No. Then I realized that I was not alone; I was in the book; I was with the characters. I was with my Self.

Not only do I not feel alone with my characters; they are more vivid and interesting to me than the people in my real life. If you think about it, the case can't be otherwise. In order for a book (or any project or enterprise) to hold our attention for the length of time it takes to unfold itself, it has to plug into some internal perplexity or passion that is of paramount importance to us. That problem becomes the theme of our work, even if we can't at the start understand or articulate it. As the characters arise, each embodies infallibly an aspect of that dilemma, that perplexity. These characters might not be interesting to anyone else but they're absolutely fascinating to us. They are us. Meaner, smarter, sexier versions of ourselves. It's fun to be with them because they're wrestling with the same issue that has its hooks into us. They're our soul mates, our lovers, our best friends. Even the villains. Especially the villains.

Even in a book like this, which has no characters, I don't feel alone because I'm imagining the reader, whom I conjure as an aspiring artist much like my own younger, less grizzled self, to whom I hope to impart a little starch and inspiration and prime, a little, with some hard-knocks wisdom and a few tricks of the trade.

RESISTANCE AND HEALING

Have you ever spent time in Santa Fe? There's a subculture of "healing" there. The idea is that there's something therapeutic in the atmosphere. A safe place to go and get yourself together. There are other places (Santa Barbara and Ojai, California, come to mind), usually populated by upper-middle-class people with more time and money than they know what to do with, in which a culture of healing also obtains. The concept in all these environments seems to be that one needs to complete his healing before he is ready to do his work.

This way of thinking (are you ahead of me?) is a form of Resistance.

What are we trying to heal, anyway? The athlete knows the day will never come when he wakes up pain-free. He has to play hurt.

Remember, the part of us that we imagine needs healing is not the part we create from; that part is far deeper and stronger. The part we create from can't be touched by anything our parents did, or society did. That part is unsullied, uncorrupted; soundproof, waterproof, and bulletproof. In fact, the more troubles we've got, the better and richer that part becomes.

The part that needs healing is our personal life. Personal life has nothing to do with work. Besides, what better way of healing than to find our center of self-sovereignty? Isn't that the whole point of healing?

I washed up in New York a couple of decades ago, making twenty bucks a night driving a cab and running away full-time from doing my work. One night, alone in my $110-a-month sublet, I hit bottom in terms of having diverted myself into so many phony channels so many times that I couldn't rationalize it for one more evening. I dragged out my ancient Smith-Corona, dreading the experience as pointless, fruitless, meaningless, not to say the most painful exercise I could think of. For two hours I made myself sit there, torturing out some trash that I chucked immediately into the shitcan. That was enough. I put the machine away. I went back to the kitchen. In the sink sat ten days of dishes. For some reason I had enough excess energy that I decided to wash them. The warm water felt pretty good. The soap and sponge were doing their thing. A pile of clean plates began rising in the drying rack. To my amazement I realized I was whistling.

It hit me that I had turned a corner.

I was okay.

I would be okay from here on.

Do you understand? I hadn't written anything good. It

might be years before I would, if I ever did at all. That didn't matter. What counted was that I had, after years of running from it, actually sat down and done my work.

Don't get me wrong. I've got nothing against true healing. We all need it. But it has nothing to do with doing our work and it can be a colossal exercise in Resistance. Resistance loves "healing." Resistance knows that the more psychic energy we expend dredging and re-dredging the tired, boring injustices of our personal lives, the less juice we have to do our work.

RESISTANCE AND SUPPORT

H ave you ever been to a workshop? These boondoggles are colleges of Resistance. They ought to give out Ph.D.'s in Resistance. What better way of avoiding work than going to a workshop? But what I hate even worse is the word *support*.

Seeking support from friends and family is like having your people gathered around at your deathbed. It's nice, but when the ship sails, all they can do is stand on the dock waving goodbye.

Any support we get from persons of flesh and blood is like Monopoly money; it's not legal tender in that sphere where we have to do our work. In fact, the more energy we spend stoking up on support from colleagues and loved ones, the weaker we become and the less capable of handling our business.

My friend Carol had the following dream, at a time when her life felt like it was careening out of control:

She was a passenger on a bus. Bruce Springsteen was driving. Suddenly Springsteen pulled over, handed Carol the keys, and bolted. In the dream Carol was panicking. How could she drive this huge rolling Greyhound? By now all the passengers were staring. Clearly no one else was gonna step forward and take charge. Carol took the wheel. To her amazement, she found she could handle it.

Later, analyzing the dream, she figured Bruce Springsteen was "The Boss." The boss of her psyche. The bus was the vehicle of her life. The Boss was telling Carol it was time to take the wheel. More than that, the dream, by actually setting her down in the driver's seat and letting her feel that she could control the vehicle on the road, was providing her with a simulator run, to prime her with the confidence that she could actually take command in her life.

A dream like that is real support. It's a check you can cash when you sit down, alone, to do your work.

P.S. When your deeper Self delivers a dream like that, don't talk about it. Don't dilute its power. The dream is for you. It's between you and your Muse. Shut up and use it.

The only exception is, you may share it with another comrade-in-arms, if sharing it will help or encourage that comrade in his or her own endeavors.

RESISTANCE AND RATIONALIZATION

R ationalization is Resistance's right-hand man. Its job is to keep us from feeling the shame we would feel if we truly faced what cowards we are for not doing our work.

> **MICHAEL**
> Don't knock rationalization. Where would we be without it? I don't know anyone who can get through the day without two or three juicy rationalizations. They're more important than sex.

> **SAM**
> Aw, come on! Nothing's more important than sex.

> **MICHAEL**
> Oh yeah? Have you ever gone a week without a rationalization?

—Jeff Goldblum and Tom Berenger,
in Lawrence Kasdan's *The Big Chill*

But rationalization has its own sidekick. It's that part of our psyche that actually believes what rationalization tells us.

It's one thing to lie to ourselves. It's another thing to believe it.

RESISTANCE AND
RATIONALIZATION,
PART TWO

Resistance is fear. But Resistance is too cunning to show itself naked in this form. Why? Because if Resistance lets us see clearly that our own fear is preventing us from doing our work, we may feel shame at this. And shame may drive us to act in the face of fear.

Resistance doesn't want us to do this. So it brings in Rationalization. Rationalization is Resistance's spin doctor. It's Resistance's way of hiding the Big Stick behind its back. Instead of showing us our fear (which might shame us and impel us to do our work), Resistance presents us with a series of plausible, rational justifications for why we shouldn't do our work.

What's particularly insidious about the rationalizations that Resistance presents to us is that a lot of them are true. They're legitimate. Our wife may really be in her eighth month of pregnancy; she may in truth need us at home. Our department may really be instituting a changeover that will eat up hours of our time. Indeed it may make sense to put off finishing our dissertation, at least till after the baby's born.

What Resistance leaves out, of course, is that all this means diddly. Tolstoy had thirteen kids and wrote

War and Peace. Lance Armstrong had cancer and won the Tour de France three years and counting.

RESISTANCE CAN BE BEATEN

I f Resistance couldn't be beaten, there would be no Fifth Symphony, no *Romeo and Juliet*, no Golden Gate Bridge. Defeating Resistance is like giving birth. It seems absolutely impossible until you remember that women have been pulling it off successfully, with support and without, for fifty million years.

BOOK TWO

COMBATING RESISTANCE

Turning Pro

It is one thing to study war
and another to live the warrior's life.

—Telamon of Arcadia,
mercenary of the fifth century B.C.

PROFESSIONALS AND AMATEURS

A spiring artists defeated by Resistance share one trait. They all think like amateurs. They have not yet turned pro.

The moment an artist turns pro is as epochal as the birth of his first child. With one stroke, everything changes. I can state absolutely that the term of my life can be divided into two parts: before turning pro, and after.

To be clear: When I say professional, I don't mean doctors and lawyers, those of "the professions." I mean the Professional as an ideal. The professional in contrast to the amateur. Consider the differences.

The amateur plays for fun. The professional plays for keeps.

To the amateur, the game is his avocation. To the pro it's his vocation.

The amateur plays part-time, the professional full-time.

The amateur is a weekend warrior. The professional is there seven days a week.

The word *amateur* comes from the Latin root meaning "to love." The conventional interpretation is that the amateur pursues his calling out of love, while the pro does it for money. Not the way I see it. In my view, the amateur does not love the game enough. If he did, he would not pursue it as a sideline, distinct from his "real" vocation.

The professional loves it so much he dedicates his life to it. He commits full-time.

That's what I mean when I say turning pro.

Resistance hates it when we turn pro.

A PROFESSIONAL

Someone once asked Somerset Maugham if he wrote on a schedule or only when struck by inspiration. "I write only when inspiration strikes," he replied. "Fortunately it strikes every morning at nine o'clock sharp."

That's a pro.

In terms of Resistance, Maugham was saying, "I despise Resistance; I will not let it faze me; I will sit down and do my work."

Maugham reckoned another, deeper truth: that by performing the mundane physical act of sitting down and starting to work, he set in motion a mysterious but infallible sequence of events that would produce inspiration, as surely as if the goddess had synchronized her watch with his.

He knew if he built it, she would come.

WHAT A WRITER'S DAY FEELS LIKE

I wake up with a gnawing sensation of dissatisfaction. Already I feel fear. Already the loved ones around me are starting to fade. I interact. I'm present. But I'm not.

I'm not thinking about the work. I've already consigned that to the Muse. What I am aware of is Resistance. I feel it in my guts. I afford it the utmost respect, because I know it can defeat me on any given day as easily as the need for a drink can overcome an alcoholic.

I go through the chores, the correspondence, the obligations of daily life. Again I'm there but not really. The clock is running in my head; I know I can indulge in daily crap for a little while, but I must cut it off when the bell rings.

I'm keenly aware of the Principle of Priority, which states (a) you must know the difference between what is urgent and what is important, and (b) you must do what's important first.

What's important is the work. That's the game I have to suit up for. That's the field on which I have to leave everything I've got.

Do I really believe that my work is crucial to the planet's survival? Of course not. But it's as important to me as catching that mouse is to the hawk circling outside my window. He's hungry. He needs a kill. So do I.

I'm done with my chores now. It's time. I say my prayer and head out on the hunt.

The sun isn't up yet; it's cold; the fields are sopping. Brambles scratch my ankles, branches snap back in my face. The hill is a sonofabitch but what can you do? Set one foot in front of another and keep climbing.

An hour passes. I'm warmer now, the pace has got my blood going. The years have taught me one skill: how to be miserable. I know how to shut up and keep humping. This is a great asset because it's human, the proper role for a mortal. It does not offend the gods, but elicits their intercession. My bitching self is receding now. The instincts are taking over. Another hour passes. I turn the corner of a thicket and there he is: the nice fat hare I knew would show up if I just kept plugging.

Home from the hill, I thank the immortals and offer up their portion of the kill. They brought it to me; they deserve their share. I am grateful.

I joke with my kids beside the fire. They're happy; the old man has brought home the bacon. The old lady's happy; she's cooking it up. I'm happy; I've earned my keep on the planet, at least for this day.

Resistance is not a factor now. I don't think of the hunt and I don't think of the office. The tension drains from my neck and back. What I feel and say and do this night will not be coming from any disowned or unresolved part of me, any part corrupted by Resistance.

I go to sleep content, but my final thought is of Resistance. I will wake up with it tomorrow. Already I am steeling myself.

HOW TO BE MISERABLE

In my younger days dodging the draft, I somehow wound up in the Marine Corps. There's a myth that Marine training turns baby-faced recruits into bloodthirsty killers. Trust me, the Marine Corps is not that efficient. What it does teach, however, is a lot more useful.

The Marine Corps teaches you how to be miserable.

This is invaluable for an artist.

Marines love to be miserable. Marines derive a perverse satisfaction in having colder chow, crappier equipment, and higher casualty rates than any outfit of dogfaces, swab jockeys, or flyboys, all of whom they despise. Why? Because these candy-asses don't know how to be miserable.

The artist committing himself to his calling has volunteered for hell, whether he knows it or not. He will be dining for the duration on a diet of isolation, rejection, self-doubt, despair, ridicule, contempt, and humiliation.

The artist must be like that Marine. He has to know how to be miserable. He has to love being miserable. He has to take pride in being more miserable than any soldier or swabbie or jet jockey. Because this is war, baby. And war is hell.

WE'RE ALL PROS ALREADY

All of us are pros in one area: our jobs.

We get a paycheck. We work for money. We are professionals.

Now: Are there principles we can take from what we're already successfully doing in our workaday life and apply to our artistic aspirations? What exactly are the qualities that define us as professionals?

1) *We show up every day.* We might do it only because we have to, to keep from getting fired. But we do it. We show up every day.

2) *We show up no matter what.* In sickness and in health, come hell or high water, we stagger in to the factory. We might do it only so as not to let down our co-workers, or for other, less noble reasons. But we do it. We show up no matter what.

3) *We stay on the job all day.* Our minds may wander, but our bodies remain at the wheel. We pick up the phone when it rings, we assist the customer when he seeks our help. We don't go home till the whistle blows.

4) *We are committed over the long haul.* Next year we may go to another job, another company, another country. But we'll still be working. Until we hit the lottery, we are part of the labor force.

5) *The stakes for us are high and real.* This is about survival, feeding our families, educating our children. It's about eating.

6) *We accept remuneration for our labor.* We're not here for fun. We work for money.

7) *We do not overidentify with our jobs.* We may take pride in our work, we may stay late and come in on weekends, but we recognize that we are not our job descriptions. The amateur, on the other hand, overidentifies with his avocation, his artistic aspiration. He defines himself by it. He is a musician, a painter, a playwright. Resistance loves this. Resistance knows that the amateur composer will never write his symphony because he is overly invested in its success and overterrified of its failure. The amateur takes it so seriously it paralyzes him.

8) *We master the technique of our jobs.*

9) *We have a sense of humor about our jobs.*

10) *We receive praise or blame in the real world.*

Now consider the amateur: the aspiring painter, the wannabe playwright. How does he pursue his calling?

One, he doesn't show up every day. Two, he doesn't show up no matter what. Three, he doesn't stay on the job all day. He is not committed over the long haul; the stakes for him are illusory and fake. He does not get money. And he overidentifies with his art. He does not have a sense of humor about failure. You don't hear him bitching, "This fucking trilogy is killing me!" Instead, he doesn't write his trilogy at all.

The amateur has not mastered the technique of his art. Nor does he expose himself to judgment in the real world. If we show our poem to our friend and our friend says, "It's wonderful, I love it," that's not real-world feedback, that's our friend being nice to us. Nothing is as empowering as real-world validation, even if it's for failure.

The first professional writing job I ever had, after seventeen years of trying, was on a movie called *King Kong Lives*. I and my partner-at-the-time, Ron Shusett (a brilliant writer and producer who also did *Alien* and *Total Recall*) hammered out the screenplay for Dino DeLaurentiis. We loved it; we were sure we had a hit. Even after we'd seen the finished film, we were certain it was a blockbuster. We invited everyone we knew to the premiere, even rented out the joint next door for a post-triumph blowout. Get there early, we warned our friends, the place'll be mobbed.

Nobody showed. There was only one guy in line beside our guests and he was muttering something about spare change. In the theater, our friends endured the movie in mute stupefaction. When the lights came up, they fled like cockroaches into the night.

Next day came the review in *Variety*: ". . . Ronald Shusett and Steven Pressfield; we hope these are not their real names, for their parents' sake." When the first week's grosses came in, the flick barely registered. Still I clung to hope. Maybe it's only tanking in urban areas, maybe it's playing better in the burbs. I motored to an Edge City multiplex. A youth manned the popcorn booth. "How's *King Kong Lives?*" I asked. He flashed thumbs-down. "Miss it, man. It sucks."

I was crushed. Here I was, forty-two years old, divorced, childless, having given up all normal human pursuits to chase the dream of being a writer; now I've finally got my name on a big-time Hollywood production starring Linda Hamilton, and what happens? I'm a loser, a phony; my life is worthless, and so am I.

My friend Tony Keppelman snapped me out of it by asking if I was gonna quit. Hell, no! "Then be happy. You're where you wanted to be, aren't you? So you're taking a few blows. That's the price for being in the arena and not on the sidelines. Stop complaining and be grateful."

That was when I realized I had become a pro. I had not yet had a success. But I had had a real failure.

FOR LOVE OF THE GAME

To clarify a point about professionalism: The professional, though he accepts money, does his work out of love. He has to love it. Otherwise he wouldn't devote his life to it of his own free will.

The professional has learned, however, that too much love can be a bad thing. Too much love can make him choke. The seeming detachment of the professional, the cold-blooded character to his demeanor, is a compensating device to keep him from loving the game so much that he freezes in action. Playing for money, or adopting the attitude of one who plays for money, lowers the fever.

Remember what we said about fear, love, and Resistance. The more you love your art/calling/enterprise, the more important its accomplishment is to the evolution of your soul, the more you will fear it and the more Resistance you will experience facing it. The payoff of playing-the-game-for-money is not the money (which you may never see anyway, even after you turn pro). The payoff is that playing the game for money produces the proper professional attitude. It inculcates the lunch-pail mentality, the hard-core, hard-head, hard-hat state of mind that shows up for work despite rain or snow or dark of night and slugs it out day after day.

The writer is an infantryman. He knows that progress is measured in yards of dirt extracted from the enemy one day, one hour, one minute at a time and paid for in blood. The artist wears combat boots. He looks in the mirror and sees GI Joe. Remember, the Muse favors working stiffs. She hates prima donnas. To the gods the supreme sin is not rape or murder, but pride. To think of yourself as a mercenary, a gun for hire, implants the proper humility. It purges pride and preciousness.

Resistance loves pride and preciousness. Resistance says, "Show me a writer who's too good to take Job X or Assignment Y and I'll show you a guy I can crack like a walnut."

Technically, the professional takes money. Technically, the pro plays for pay. But in the end, he does it for love.

Now let's consider: What are the aspects of the Professional?

A PROFESSIONAL IS PATIENT

Resistance outwits the amateur with the oldest trick in the book: It uses his own enthusiasm against him. Resistance gets us to plunge into a project with an overambitious and unrealistic timetable for its completion. It knows we can't sustain that level of intensity. We will hit the wall. We will crash.

The professional, on the other hand, understands delayed gratification. He is the ant, not the grasshopper; the tortoise, not the hare. Have you heard the legend of Sylvester Stallone staying up three nights straight to churn out the screenplay for *Rocky?* I don't know, it may even be true. But it's the most pernicious species of myth to set before the awakening writer, because it seduces him into believing he can pull off the big score without pain and without persistence.

The professional arms himself with patience, not only to give the stars time to align in his career, but to keep himself from flaming out in each individual work. He knows that any job, whether it's a novel or a kitchen remodel, takes twice as long as he thinks and costs twice as much. He accepts that. He recognizes it as reality.

The professional steels himself at the start of a project,

reminding himself it is the Iditarod, not the sixty-yard dash. He conserves his energy. He prepares his mind for the long haul. He sustains himself with the knowledge that if he can just keep those huskies mushing, sooner or later the sled will pull in to Nome.

A PROFESSIONAL SEEKS ORDER

When I lived in the back of my Chevy van, I had to dig my typewriter out from beneath layers of tire tools, dirty laundry, and moldering paperbacks. My truck was a nest, a hive, a hellhole on wheels whose sleeping surface I had to clear each night just to carve out a foxhole to snooze in.

The professional cannot live like that. He is on a mission. He will not tolerate disorder. He eliminates chaos from his world in order to banish it from his mind. He wants the carpet vacuumed and the threshold swept, so the Muse may enter and not soil her gown.

A PROFESSIONAL DEMYSTIFIES

A pro views her work as craft, not art. Not because she believes art is devoid of a mystical dimension. On the contrary. She understands that all creative endeavor is holy, but she doesn't dwell on it. She knows if she thinks about that too much, it will paralyze her. So she concentrates on technique. The professional masters how, and leaves what and why to the gods. Like Somerset Maugham she doesn't wait for inspiration, she acts in the anticipation of its apparition. The professional is acutely aware of the intangibles that go into inspiration. Out of respect for them, she lets them work. She grants them their sphere while she concentrates on hers.

The sign of the amateur is overglorification of and preoccupation with the mystery.

The professional shuts up. She doesn't talk about it. She does her work.

A PROFESSIONAL ACTS IN THE FACE OF FEAR

The amateur believes he must first overcome his fear; then he can do his work. The professional knows that fear can never be overcome. He knows there is no such thing as a fearless warrior or a dread-free artist.

What Henry Fonda does, after puking into the toilet in his dressing room, is to clean up and march out onstage. He's still terrified but he forces himself forward in spite of his terror. He knows that once he gets out into the action, his fear will recede and he'll be okay.

A PROFESSIONAL
ACCEPTS NO EXCUSES

The amateur, underestimating Resistance's cunning, permits the flu to keep him from his chapters; he believes the serpent's voice in his head that says mailing off that manuscript is more important than doing the day's work.

The professional has learned better. He respects Resistance. He knows if he caves in today, no matter how plausible the pretext, he'll be twice as likely to cave in tomorrow.

The professional knows that Resistance is like a telemarketer; if you so much as say hello, you're finished. The pro doesn't even pick up the phone. He stays at work.

A PROFESSIONAL
PLAYS IT AS IT LAYS

My friend the Hawk and I were playing the first hole at Prestwick in Scotland; the wind was howling out of the left. I started an eight-iron thirty yards to windward, but the gale caught it; I watched in dismay as the ball sailed hard right, hit the green going sideways, and bounded off into the cabbage. "Sonofabitch!" I turned to our caddie. "Did you see the wind take that shot!?"

He gave that look that only Scottish caddies can give. "Well, ye've got t' play th' wind now, don't ye?"

The professional conducts his business in the real world. Adversity, injustice, bad hops and rotten calls, even good breaks and lucky bounces all comprise the ground over which the campaign must be waged. The field is level, the professional understands, only in heaven.

A PROFESSIONAL IS PREPARED

I'm not talking about craft; that goes without saying. The professional is prepared at a deeper level. He is prepared, each day, to confront his own self-sabotage.

The professional understands that Resistance is fertile and ingenious. It will throw stuff at him that he's never seen before.

The professional prepares mentally to absorb blows and to deliver them. His aim is to take what the day gives him. He is prepared to be prudent and prepared to be reckless, to take a beating when he has to, and to go for the throat when he can. He understands that the field alters every day. His goal is not victory (success will come by itself when it wants to) but to handle himself, his insides, as sturdily and steadily as he can.

A PROFESSIONAL
DOES NOT SHOW OFF

A professional's work has style; it is distinctively his own. But he doesn't let his signature grandstand for him. His style serves the material. He does not impose it as a means of drawing attention to himself.

This doesn't mean that the professional doesn't throw down a 360 tomahawk jam from time to time, just to let the boys know he's still in business.

A PROFESSIONAL
DEDICATES HIMSELF
TO MASTERING TECHNIQUE

The professional respects his craft. He does not consider himself superior to it. He recognizes the contributions of those who have gone before him. He apprentices himself to them.

The professional dedicates himself to mastering technique not because he believes technique is a substitute for inspiration but because he wants to be in possession of the full arsenal of skills when inspiration does come. The professional is sly. He knows that by toiling beside the front door of technique, he leaves room for genius to enter by the back.

A PROFESSIONAL
DOES NOT HESITATE
TO ASK FOR HELP

Tiger Woods is the greatest golfer in the world. Yet he has a teacher; he works with Butch Harmon. And Tiger doesn't endure this instruction or suffer through it—he revels in it. It's his keenest professional joy to get out there on the practice tee with Butch, to learn more about the game he loves.

Tiger Woods is the consummate professional. It would never occur to him, as it would to an amateur, that he knows everything, or can figure everything out on his own. On the contrary, he seeks out the most knowledgeable teacher and listens with both ears. The student of the game knows that the levels of revelation that can unfold in golf, as in any art, are inexhaustible.

A PROFESSIONAL
DISTANCES HERSELF
FROM HER INSTRUMENT

The pro stands at one remove from her instrument—meaning her person, her body, her voice, her talent; the physical, mental, emotional, and psychological being she uses in her work. She does not identify with this instrument. It is simply what God gave her, what she has to work with. She assesses it coolly, impersonally, objectively.

The professional identifies with her consciousness and her will, not with the matter that her consciousness and will manipulate to serve her art. Does Madonna walk around the house in cone bras and come-fuck-me bustiers? She's too busy planning D-Day. Madonna does not identify with "Madonna." Madonna employs "Madonna."

A PROFESSIONAL
DOES NOT TAKE FAILURE
(OR SUCCESS) PERSONALLY

When people say an artist has a thick skin, what they mean is not that the person is dense or numb, but that he has seated his professional consciousness in a place other than his personal ego. It takes tremendous strength of character to do this, because our deepest instincts run counter to it. Evolution has programmed us to feel rejection in our guts. This is how the tribe enforced obedience, by wielding the threat of expulsion. Fear of rejection isn't just psychological; it's biological. It's in our cells.

Resistance knows this and uses it against us. It uses fear of rejection to paralyze us and prevent us, if not from doing our work, then from exposing it to public evaluation. I had a dear friend who had labored for years on an excellent and deeply personal novel. It was done. He had it in its mailing box. But he couldn't make himself send it off. Fear of rejection unmanned him.

The professional cannot take rejection personally because to do so reinforces Resistance. Editors are not the enemy; critics are not the enemy. Resistance is the enemy. The battle is inside our own heads. We cannot let external criticism, even if it's true, fortify our internal foe. That foe is strong enough already.

A professional schools herself to stand apart from her performance, even as she gives herself to it heart and soul. *The Bhagavad-Gita* tells us we have a right only to our labor, not to the fruits of our labor. All the warrior can give is his life; all the athlete can do is leave everything on the field.

The professional loves her work. She is invested in it wholeheartedly. But she does not forget that the work is not her. Her artistic self contains many works and many performances. Already the next is percolating inside her. The next will be better, and the one after that better still.

The professional self-validates. She is tough-minded. In the face of indifference or adulation, she assesses her stuff coldly and objectively. Where it fell short, she'll improve it. Where it triumphed, she'll make it better still. She'll work harder. She'll be back tomorrow.

The professional gives an ear to criticism, seeking to learn and grow. But she never forgets that Resistance is using criticism against her on a far more diabolical level. Resistance enlists criticism to reinforce the fifth column of fear already at work inside the artist's head, seeking to break her will and crack her dedication. The professional does not fall for this. Her resolution, before all others, remains: No matter what, I will never let Resistance beat me.

A PROFESSIONAL
ENDURES ADVERSITY

I had been in Tinseltown five years, had finished nine screenplays on spec, none of which had sold. Finally I got a meeting with a big producer. He kept taking phone calls, even as I pitched my stuff. He had one of those headset things, so he didn't even have to pick up a receiver; the calls came in and he took them. Finally one came that was personal. "Would you mind?" he asked, indicating the door. "I need some privacy on this one." I exited. The door closed behind me. Ten minutes passed. I was standing out by the secretaries. Twenty more minutes passed. Finally the producer's door opened; he came out pulling on his jacket. "Oh, I'm so sorry!"

He had forgotten all about me.

I'm human. This hurt. I wasn't a kid either; I was in my forties, with a rap sheet of failure as long as your arm.

The professional cannot let himself take humiliation personally. Humiliation, like rejection and criticism, is the external reflection of internal Resistance.

The professional endures adversity. He lets the birdshit splash down on his slicker, remembering that it comes clean with a heavy-duty hosing. He himself, his creative center, cannot be buried, even beneath a mountain of guano. His core is bulletproof. Nothing can touch it unless he lets it.

I saw a fat happy old guy once in his Cadillac on the freeway. He had the A/C going, Pointer Sisters on the CD, puffing on a stogie. His license plate:

DUES PD

The professional keeps his eye on the doughnut and not on the hole. He reminds himself it's better to be in the arena, getting stomped by the bull, than to be up in the stands or out in the parking lot.

A PROFESSIONAL SELF-VALIDATES

An amateur lets the negative opinion of others unman him. He takes external criticism to heart, allowing it to trump his own belief in himself and his work. Resistance loves this.

Can you stand another Tiger Woods story? With four holes to go on the final day of the 2001 Masters (which Tiger went on to win, completing the all-four-majors-at-one-time Slam), some chucklehead in the gallery snapped a camera shutter at the top of Tiger's backswing. Incredibly, Tiger was able to pull up in mid-swing and back off the shot. But that wasn't the amazing part. After looking daggers at the malefactor, Tiger recomposed himself, stepped back to the ball, and striped it 310 down the middle.

That's a professional. It is tough-mindedness at a level most of us can't comprehend, let alone emulate. But let's look more closely at what Tiger did, or rather what he didn't do.

First, he didn't react reflexively. He didn't allow an act that by all rights should have provoked an automatic response of rage to actually produce that rage. He controlled his reaction. He governed his emotion.

Second, he didn't take it personally. He could have

perceived this shutterbug's act as a deliberate blow aimed at him individually, with the intention of throwing him off his shot. He could have reacted with outrage or indignation or cast himself as a victim. He didn't.

Third, he didn't take it as a sign of heaven's malevolence. He could have experienced this bolt as the malice of the golfing gods, like a bad hop in baseball or a linesman's miscall in tennis. He could have groaned or sulked or surrendered mentally to this injustice, this interference, and used it as an excuse to fail. He didn't.

What he did do was maintain his sovereignty over the moment. He understood that, no matter what blow had befallen him from an outside agency, he himself still had his job to do, the shot he needed to hit right here, right now. And he knew that it remained within his power to produce that shot. Nothing stood in his way except whatever emotional upset he himself chose to hold on to. Tiger's mother, Kultida, is a Buddhist. Perhaps from her he had learned compassion, to let go of fury at the heedlessness of an overzealous shutter-clicker. In any event Tiger Woods, the ultimate professional, vented his anger quickly with a look, then recomposed himself and returned to the task at hand.

The professional cannot allow the actions of others to define his reality. Tomorrow morning the critic will be gone, but the writer will still be there facing the blank page. Nothing matters but that he keep working. Short of a family crisis or the outbreak of World War III, the professional shows up, ready to serve the gods.

Remember, Resistance wants us to cede sovereignty to others. It wants us to stake our self-worth, our identity, our reason-for-being, on the response of others to our work. Resistance knows we can't take this. No one can.

The professional blows critics off. He doesn't even hear them. Critics, he reminds himself, are the unwitting mouth-pieces of Resistance and as such can be truly cunning and pernicious. They can articulate in their reviews the same toxic venom that Resistance itself concocts inside our heads. That is their real evil. Not that we believe them, but that we believe the Resistance in our own minds, for which critics serve as unconscious spokespersons.

The professional learns to recognize envy-driven criticism and to take it for what it is: the supreme compliment. The critic hates most that which he would have done himself if he had had the guts.

A PROFESSIONAL
RECOGNIZES HER LIMITATIONS

She gets an agent, she gets a lawyer, she gets an accountant. She knows she can only be a professional at one thing. She brings in other pros and treats them with respect.

A PROFESSIONAL
REINVENTS HIMSELF

G oldie Hawn once observed that there are only three ages for an actress in Hollywood: "Babe, D.A., and Driving Miss Daisy." She was making a different point, but the truth remains: As artists we serve the Muse, and the Muse may have more than one job for us over our lifetime.

The professional does not permit himself to become hidebound within one incarnation, however comfortable or successful. Like a transmigrating soul, he shucks his outworn body and dons a new one. He continues his journey.

A PROFESSIONAL IS RECOGNIZED
BY OTHER PROFESSIONALS

The professional senses who has served his time and who hasn't. Like Alan Ladd and Jack Palance circling each other in *Shane*, a gun recognizes another gun.

YOU, INC.

When I first moved to Los Angeles and made the acquaintance of working screenwriters, I learned that many had their own corporations. They provided their writing services not as themselves but as "loan-outs" from their one-man businesses. Their writing contracts were f/s/o—"for services of "—themselves. I had never seen this before. I thought it was pretty cool.

For a writer to incorporate himself has certain tax and financial advantages. But what I love about it is the metaphor. I like the idea of being Myself, Inc. That way I can wear two hats. I can hire myself and fire myself. I can even, as Robin Williams once remarked of writer-producers, blow smoke up my own ass.

Making yourself a corporation (or just thinking of yourself in that way) reinforces the idea of professionalism because it separates the artist-doing-the-work from the will-and-consciousness-running-the-show. No matter how much abuse is heaped on the head of the former, the latter takes it in stride and keeps on trucking. Conversely with success: You-the-writer may get a swelled head, but you-the-boss remember how to take yourself down a peg.

Have you ever worked in an office? Then you know about Monday morning status meetings. The group assembles in the conference room and the boss goes over what assignments each team member is responsible for in the coming week. When the meeting breaks up, an assistant prepares a work sheet and distributes it. When this hits your desk an hour later, you know exactly what you have to do that week.

I have one of those meetings with myself every Monday. I sit down and go over my assignments. Then I type it up and distribute it to myself.

I have corporate stationery and corporate business cards and a corporate checkbook. I write off corporate expenses and pay corporate taxes. I have different credit cards for myself and my corporation.

If we think of ourselves as a corporation, it gives us a healthy distance on ourselves. We're less subjective. We don't take blows as personally. We're more cold-blooded; we can price our wares more realistically. Sometimes, as Joe Blow himself, I'm too mild-mannered to go out and sell. But as Joe Blow, Inc., I can pimp the hell out of myself. I'm not me anymore. I'm Me, Inc.

I'm a pro.

A CRITTER THAT KEEPS COMING

Why does Resistance yield to our turning pro? Because Resistance is a bully. Resistance has no strength of its own; its power derives entirely from our fear of it. A bully will back down before the runtiest twerp who stands his ground.

The essence of professionalism is the focus upon the work and its demands, while we are doing it, to the exclusion of all else. The ancient Spartans schooled themselves to regard the enemy, any enemy, as nameless and faceless. In other words, they believed that if they did their work, no force on earth could stand against them. In *The Searchers*, John Wayne and Jeffrey Hunter pursue the war chief, Scar, who has kidnapped their young kinswoman, played by Natalie Wood. Winter stops them, but Wayne's character, Ethan Edwards, does not slacken his resolve. He'll return to the trail in spring, he declares, and, sooner or later, the fugitive's vigilance will slacken.

ETHAN

```
Seems he never learns there's such a thing
as a critter that might just keep comin' on.
So we'll find 'em in the end, I promise you that.
Just as sure as the turning of the earth.
```

The pro keeps coming on. He beats Resistance at its own game by being even more resolute and even more implacable than it is.

NO MYSTERY

There's no mystery to turning pro. It's a decision brought about by an act of will. We make up our mind to view ourselves as pros and we do it. Simple as that.

BOOK THREE

BEYOND RESISTANCE

The Higher Realm

The first duty is to sacrifice to the gods and pray them to grant you the thoughts, words, and deeds likely to render your command most pleasing to the gods and to bring yourself, your friends, and your city the fullest measure of affection and glory and advantage.

–Xenophon,
The Cavalry Commander

ANGELS IN THE ABSTRACT

The next few chapters are going to be about those invisible psychic forces that support and sustain us in our journey toward ourselves. I plan on using terms like *muses* and *angels*.

Does that make you uncomfortable?

If it does, you have my permission to think of angels in the abstract. Consider these forces as being impersonal as gravity. Maybe they are. It's not hard to believe, is it, that a force exists in every grain and seed to make it grow? Or that in every kitten or colt is an instinct that impels it to run and play and learn.

Just as Resistance can be thought of as personal (I've said Resistance "loves" such-and-such or "hates" such-and-such), it can also be viewed as a force of nature as impersonal as entropy or molecular decay.

Similarly the call to growth can be conceptualized as personal (a *daimon* or *genius,* an angel or a muse) or as impersonal, like the tides or the transiting of Venus. Either way works, as long as we're comfortable with it. Or if extra-dimensionality doesn't sit well with you in any form, think of it as "talent," programmed into our genes by evolution.

The point, for the thesis I'm seeking to put forward, is that there are forces we can call our allies.

As Resistance works to keep us from becoming who we were born to be, equal and opposite powers are counter-poised against it. These are our allies and angels.

APPROACHING THE MYSTERY

W hy have I stressed professionalism so heavily in the preceding chapters? Because the most important thing about art is to work. Nothing else matters except sitting down every day and trying.

Why is this so important?

Because when we sit down day after day and keep grinding, something mysterious starts to happen. A process is set into motion by which, inevitably and infallibly, heaven comes to our aid. Unseen forces enlist in our cause; serendipity reinforces our purpose.

This is the other secret that real artists know and wannabe writers don't. When we sit down each day and do our work, power concentrates around us. The Muse takes note of our dedication. She approves. We have earned favor in her sight. When we sit down and work, we become like a magnetized rod that attracts iron filings. Ideas come. Insights accrete.

Just as Resistance has its seat in hell, so Creation has its home in heaven. And it's not just a witness, but an eager and active ally.

What I call Professionalism someone else might call the Artist's Code or the Warrior's Way. It's an attitude of egolessness and service. The Knights of the Round Table were chaste and self-effacing. Yet they dueled dragons.

We're facing dragons too. Fire-breathing griffins of the soul, whom we must outfight and outwit to reach the treasure of our self-in-potential and to release the maiden who is God's plan and destiny for ourselves and the answer to why we were put on this planet.

INVOKING THE MUSE

The quote from Xenophon that opens this section comes from a pamphlet called *The Cavalry Commander*, in which the celebrated warrior and historian proffers instruction to those young gentlemen who aspired to be officers of the Athenian equestrian corps. He declares that the commander's first duty, before he mucks out a stable or seeks funding from the Defense Review Board, is to sacrifice to the gods and invoke their aid.

I do the same thing. The last thing I do before I sit down to work is say my prayer to the Muse. I say it out loud, in absolute earnest. Only then do I get down to business.

In my late twenties I rented a little house in Northern California; I had gone there to finish a novel or kill myself trying. By that time I had blown up a marriage to a girl I loved with all my heart, screwed up two careers, blah blah, etc., all because (though I had no understanding of this at the time) I could not handle Resistance. I had one novel nine-tenths of the way through and another at ninety-nine hundredths before I threw them in the trash. I couldn't finish 'em. I didn't have the guts. In yielding thusly to Resistance, I fell prey to every vice, evil, distraction, you-name-it mentioned heretofore, all leading nowhere, and finally washed up in this sleepy California town, with my Chevy van, my cat Mo, and my antique Smith-Corona.

A guy named Paul Rink lived down the street. Look him up, he's in Henry Miller's *Big Sur and the Oranges of Hieronymus Bosch*. Paul was a writer. He lived in his camper, "Moby Dick." I started each day over coffee with Paul. He turned me on to all kinds of authors I had never heard of, lectured me on self-discipline, dedication, the evils of the marketplace. But best of all, he shared with me his prayer, the Invocation of the Muse from Homer's *Odyssey*, the T. E. Lawrence translation. Paul typed it out for me on his even-more-ancient-than-mine manual Remington. I still have it. It's yellow and parched as dust; the merest puff would blow it to powder.

In my little house I had no TV. I never read a newspaper or went to a movie. I just worked. One afternoon I was banging away in the little bedroom I had converted to an office, when I heard my neighbor's radio playing outside. Someone in a loud voice was declaiming ". . . to preserve, protect, and defend the Constitution of the United States." I came out. What's going on? "Didn't you hear? Nixon's out; they got a new guy in there."

I had missed Watergate completely.

I was determined to keep working. I had failed so many times, and caused myself and people I loved so much pain thereby, that I felt if I crapped out this time I would have to hang myself. I didn't know what Resistance was then. No one had schooled me in the concept. I felt it though, big-time. I experienced it as a compulsion to self-destruct. I could not finish what I started. The closer I got, the more different ways I'd find to screw it up. I worked for twenty-six months straight, taking only two out for a stint of migrant labor in Washington State, and finally one day I got to the last page and typed out:

THE END.

I never did find a buyer for the book. Or the next one, either. It was ten years before I got the first check for something I had written and ten more before a novel, *The Legend of Bagger Vance*, was actually published. But that moment when I first hit the keys to spell out THE END was epochal. I remember rolling the last page out and adding it to the stack that was the finished manuscript. Nobody knew I was done. Nobody cared. But I knew. I felt like a dragon I'd been fighting all my life had just dropped dead at my feet and gasped out its last sulfuric breath.

Rest in peace, motherfucker.

Next morning I went over to Paul's for coffee and told him I had finished. "Good for you," he said without looking up. "Start the next one today."

INVOKING THE MUSE,
PART TWO

Before I met Paul, I had never heard of the Muses. He enlightened me. The Muses were nine sisters, daughters of Zeus and Mnemosyne, which means "memory." Their names are Clio, Erato, Thalia, Terpsichore, Calliope, Polyhymnia, Euterpe, Melpomene, and Urania. Their job is to inspire artists. Each Muse is responsible for a different art. There's a neighborhood in New Orleans where the streets are named after the Muses. I lived there once and had no idea; I thought they were just weird names.

Here's Socrates, in Plato's *Phaedrus,* on the "noble effect of heaven-sent madness":

> The third type of possession and madness is possession by the Muses. When this seizes upon a gentle and virgin soul it rouses it to inspired expression in lyric and other sorts of poetry, and glorifies countless deeds of the heroes of old for the instruction of posterity. But if a man comes to the door of poetry untouched by the madness of the Muses, believing that technique alone will make him a good poet, he and his sane compositions never reach perfection, but are utterly eclipsed by the performances of the inspired madman.

The Greek way of apprehending the mystery was to personify it. The ancients sensed powerful primordial forces in the world. To make them approachable, they gave them human faces. They called them Zeus, Apollo, Aphrodite. American Indians felt the same mystery but rendered it in animistic forms—Bear Teacher, Hawk Messenger, Coyote Trickster.

Our ancestors were keenly cognizant of forces and energies whose seat was not in this material sphere but in a loftier, more mysterious one. What did they believe about this higher reality?

First, they believed that death did not exist there. The gods are immortal.

The gods, though not unlike humans, are infinitely more powerful. To defy their will is futile. To act toward heaven with pride is to call down calamity.

Time and space display an altered existence in this higher dimension. The gods travel "swift as thought." They can tell the future, some of them, and though the playwright Agathon tells us,

> This alone is denied to God:
> the power to undo the past

yet the immortals can play tricks with time, as we ourselves may sometimes, in dreams or visions.

The universe, the Greeks believed, was not indifferent. The gods take an interest in human affairs, and intercede for good or ill in our designs.

The contemporary view is that all this is charming but preposterous. Is it? Then answer this. Where did *Hamlet* come from? Where did the Parthenon come from? Where did *Nude Descending a Staircase* come from?

TESTAMENT OF A VISIONARY

Eternity is in love with the creations of time.
— William Blake

The visionary poet William Blake was, so I understand, one of those half-mad avatars who appear in flesh from time to time—savants capable of ascending for brief periods to loftier planes and returning to share the wonders they have seen.

Shall we try to decipher the meaning of the verse above?

What Blake means by "eternity," I think, is the sphere higher than this one, a plane of reality superior to the material dimension in which we dwell. In "eternity," there is no such thing as time (or Blake's syntax wouldn't distinguish it from "eternity") and probably no space either. This plane may be inhabited by higher creatures. Or it may be pure consciousness or spirit. But whatever it is, according to Blake, it's capable of being "in love."

If beings inhabit this plane, I take Blake to mean that they are incorporeal. They don't have bodies. But they have a connection to the sphere of time, the one we live in. These gods or spirits participate in this dimension. They take an interest in it.

"Eternity is in love with the creations of time" means, to me, that in some way these creatures of the higher sphere (or the sphere itself, in the abstract) take joy in what we time-bound beings can bring forth into physical existence in our limited material sphere.

It may be pushing the envelope, but if these beings take joy in the "creations of time," might they not also nudge us a little to produce them? If that's true, then the image of the Muse whispering inspiration in the artist's ear is quite apt.

The timeless communicating to the timebound.

By Blake's model, as I understand it, it's as though the Fifth Symphony existed already in that higher sphere, before Beethoven sat down and played dah-dah-dah-DUM. The catch was this: The work existed only as potential—without a body, so to speak. It wasn't music yet. You couldn't play it. You couldn't hear it.

It needed someone. It needed a corporeal being, a human, an artist (or more precisely a *genius,* in the Latin sense of "soul" or "animating spirit") to bring it into being on this material plane. So the Muse whispered in Beethoven's ear. Maybe she hummed a few bars into a million other ears. But no one else heard her. Only Beethoven got it.

He brought it forth. He made the Fifth Symphony a "creation of time," which "eternity" could be "in love with."

So that eternity, whether we conceive of it as God, pure consciousness, infinite intelligence, omniscient spirit, or if we choose to think of it as beings, gods, spirits, avatars—when "it" or "they" hear somehow the sounds of earthly music, it brings them joy.

In other words, Blake agrees with the Greeks. The gods do exist. They do penetrate our earthly sphere.

Which brings us back to the Muse. The Muse, remember, is the daughter of Zeus, Father of the Gods, and Memory, Mnemosyne. That's a pretty impressive pedigree. I'll accept those credentials.

I'll take Xenophon at his word; before I sit down to work, I'll take a minute and show respect to this unseen Power who can make or break me.

INVOKING THE MUSE,
PART THREE

Artists have invoked the Muse since time immemorial. There is great wisdom to this. There is magic to effacing our human arrogance and humbly entreating help from a source we cannot see, hear, touch, or smell. Here's the start of Homer's *Odyssey*, the T. E. Lawrence translation:

> O Divine Poesy, goddess, daughter of Zeus, sustain for me this song of the various-minded man who, after he had plundered the innermost citadel of hallowed Troy, was made to stray grievously about the coasts of men, the sport of their customs, good and bad, while his heart, through all the sea-faring, ached with an agony to redeem himself and bring his company safe home. Vain hope—for them. The fools! Their own witlessness cast them aside. To destroy for meat the oxen of the most exalted Sun, wherefore the Sun-god blotted out the day of their return. Make this tale live for us in all its many bearings, O Muse. . . .

This passage will reward closer study.

First, *Divine* Poesy. When we invoke the Muse we are calling on a force not just from a different plane of reality, but from a holier plane.

Goddess, daughter of Zeus. Not only are we invoking divine intercession, but intercession on the highest level, just one remove from the top.

Sustain for me. Homer doesn't ask for brilliance or success. He just wants to keep this thing going.

This song. That about covers it. From *The Brothers Karamazov* to your new venture in the plumbing-supply business.

I love the summation of Odysseus' trials that comprises the body of the invocation. It's Joseph Campbell's hero's journey in a nutshell, as concise a synopsis of the story of Everyman as it gets. There's the initial crime (which we all inevitably commit), which ejects the hero from his homebound complacency and propels him upon his wanderings, the yearning for redemption, the untiring campaign to get "home," meaning back to God's grace, back to himself.

I admire particularly the warning against the second crime, *to destroy for meat the oxen of the most exalted Sun.* That's the felony that calls down soul-destruction: the employment of the sacred for profane means. Prostitution. Selling out.

Lastly, the artist's wish for his work: *Make this tale live for us in all its many bearings, O Muse.*

That's what we want, isn't it? More than make it

great, make it live. And not from one angle only, but in all its many bearings.

Okay.

We've said our prayer. We're ready to work. Now what?

THE MAGIC OF MAKING A START

Concerning all acts of initiative (and creation)there is one elementary truth, the ignorance of which kills countless ideas and splendid plans: that the moment one definitely commits oneself, then providence moves too. All sorts of things occur to help one that would not otherwise have occurred. A whole stream of events issues from the decision, raising in one's favour all manner of unforeseen incidents and meetings and material assistance which no man would have dreamed would come his way. I have learned a deep respect for one of Goethe's couplets: "Whatever you can do, or dream you can, begin it. Boldness has genius, magic, and power in it. Begin it now."

—W. H. Murray,
The Scottish Himalayan Expedition

Did you ever see *Wings of Desire,* Wim Wenders's film about angels among us? (*City of Angels* with Meg Ryan and Nicolas Cage was the American version.) I believe it. I believe there are angels. They're here, but we can't see them.

Angels work for God. It's their job to help us. Wake us up. Bump us along.

Angels are agents of evolution. The Kabbalah describes angels as bundles of light, meaning intelligence, consciousness. Kabbalists believe that above every blade of grass is an angel crying "Grow! Grow!" I'll go further. I believe that above the entire human race is one super-angel, crying "Evolve! Evolve!"

Angels are like muses. They know stuff we don't. They want to help us. They're on the other side of a pane of glass, shouting to get our attention. But we can't hear them. We're too distracted by our own nonsense.

Ah, but when we begin.

When we make a start.

When we conceive an enterprise and commit to it in the face of our fears, something wonderful happens. A crack appears in the membrane. Like the first craze when a chick pecks at the inside of its shell. Angel midwives congregate around us; they assist as we give birth to ourselves, to that person we were born to be, to the one whose destiny was encoded in our soul, our *daimon,* our *genius.*

When we make a beginning, we get out of our own way

and allow the angels to come in and do their job. They can speak to us now and it makes them happy. It makes God happy. Eternity, as Blake might have told us, has opened a portal into time.

And we're it.

THE MAGIC OF KEEPING GOING

When I finish a day's work, I head up into the hills for a hike. I take a pocket tape recorder because I know that as my surface mind empties with the walk, another part of me will chime in and start talking.

> The word "leer" on page 342 . . . it should be "ogle."

> You repeated yourself in Chapter 21. The last sentence is just like that one in the middle of Chapter 7.

That's the kind of stuff that comes. It comes to all of us, every day, every minute. These paragraphs I'm writing now were dictated to me yesterday; they replace a prior, weaker opening to this chapter. I'm unspooling the new improved version now, right off the recorder.

This process of self-revision and self-correction is so common we don't even notice. But it's a miracle. And its implications are staggering.

Who's doing this revising anyway? What force is yanking at our sleeves?

What does it tell us about the architecture of our psyches

that, without our exerting effort or even thinking about it, some voice in our head pipes up to counsel us (and counsel us wisely) on how to do our work and live our lives? Whose voice is it? What software is grinding away, scanning gigabytes, while we, our mainstream selves, are otherwise occupied?

Are these angels?

Are they muses?

Is this the Unconscious?

The Self?

Whatever it is, it's smarter than we are. A lot smarter. It doesn't need us to tell it what to do. It goes to work all by itself. It seems to want to work. It seems to enjoy it.

What exactly is it doing?

It's organizing.

The principle of organization is built into nature. Chaos itself is self-organizing. Out of primordial disorder, stars find their orbits; rivers make their way to the sea.

When we, like God, set out to create a universe—a book, an opera, a new business venture—the same principle kicks in. Our screenplay resolves itself into a three-act structure; our symphony takes shape into movements; our plumbing-supply venture discovers its optimum chain of command. How do we experience this? By having ideas. Insights pop into our heads while we're shaving or taking a shower or even, amazingly, while we're actually working. The elves behind this are smart. If we forget something, they remind us. If we veer off-course, they trim the tabs and steer us back.

What can we conclude from this?

Clearly some intelligence is at work, independent of our conscious mind and yet in alliance with it, processing our material for us and alongside us.

This is why artists are modest. They know they're not doing the work; they're just taking dictation. It's also why "noncreative people" hate "creative people." Because they're jealous. They sense that artists and writers are tapped into some grid of energy and inspiration that they themselves cannot connect with.

Of course, this is nonsense. We're all creative. We all have the same psyche. The same everyday miracles are happening in all our heads day by day, minute by minute.

LARGO

I n my twenties I drove tractor-trailers for a company
called Burton Lines in Durham, North Carolina. I wasn't
very good at it; my self-destruction demons had me. Only
blind luck kept me from killing myself and any other poor
suckers who happened to be on the highway at the same time.
It was a tough period. I was broke, estranged from my wife
and my family. One night I had this dream:

> I was part of the crew of an aircraft carrier. Only the ship
> was stuck on dry land. It was still launching its jets and
> doing its thing, but it was marooned half a mile from the
> ocean. The sailors all knew how screwed up the situation
> was; they felt it as a keen and constant distress. The only
> bright spot was there was a Marine gunnery sergeant on
> board nicknamed "Largo." In the dream it seemed like the
> coolest name anyone could possibly have. Largo. I loved
> it. Largo was one of those hard-core senior noncoms like
> the Burt Lancaster character, Warden, in *From Here to
> Eternity*. The one guy on the ship who knows exactly
> what's going on, the tough old sarge who makes all the
> decisions and actually runs the show.

But where was Largo? I was standing miserably by the rail when the captain came over and started talking to me. Even he was lost. It was his ship, but he didn't know how to get it off dry land. I was nervous, finding myself in conversation with the brass, and couldn't think of a thing to say. The skipper didn't seem to notice; he just turned to me casually and said, "What the hell are we gonna do, Largo?"

I woke up electrified. I was Largo! I was the salty old Gunny. The power to take charge was in my hands; all I had to do was believe it.

Where did this dream come from? Plainly its intent was benevolent. What was its source? And what does it say about the workings of the universe that such things happen at all?

Again, we've all had dreams like that. Again, they're common as dirt. So is the sunrise. That doesn't make it any less a miracle.

Before I got to North Carolina I worked in the oilfields around Buras, Louisiana. I lived in a bunkhouse with a bunch of other transient geeks. One guy had picked up a paperback about meditation in a bookstore in New Orleans; he was teaching me how to do it. I used to go out to this dock after work and see if I could get into it. One night this came:

I was sitting cross-legged when an eagle came and landed on my shoulders. The eagle merged with me and took off flying, so that my head became its head and my arms its wings. It felt completely authentic. I could feel the air under my wings, as solid as water feels when you row in it with an oar. It was substantial. You could push off against it. So this was how birds flew! I realized that it was impossible for a bird to fall out of the sky; all it would have to do was extend its wings; the solid air would hold it up with the same power we feel when we stick our hand out the window of a moving car. I was pretty impressed with this movie that was playing in my head but I still had no idea what it meant. I asked the eagle, Hey, what am I supposed to be learning from this? A voice answered (silently): You're supposed to learn that things that you think are nothing, as weightless as air, are actually powerful substantial forces, as real and as solid as earth.

I understood. The eagle was telling me that dreams, visions, meditations such as this very one—things that I had till now disdained as fantasy and illusion—were as real and as solid as anything in my waking life.

I believed the eagle. I got the message. How could I not? I had felt the solidness of the air. I knew he was telling the truth.

Which brings us back to the question: Where did the eagle

come from? Why did he show up at just the right time to tell me just what I needed to hear?

Clearly some unseen intelligence had created him, giving him form as an eagle so that I would understand what it wanted to communicate. This intelligence was babying me along. Keeping it simple. Making its point in terms so clear and elementary that even someone as numb and asleep as I was could understand.

LIFE AND DEATH

Remember the movie *Billy Jack* starring Tom Laughlin? The film and its sequels have long since decamped to cable, but Tom Laughlin is still very much around. In addition to his movie work, he's a lecturer and author and a Jungian-schooled psychologist whose specialty is working with people who have been diagnosed with cancer. Tom Laughlin teaches and leads workshops; here's a paraphrase of something I heard him say:

The moment a person learns he's got terminal cancer, a profound shift takes place in his psyche. At one stroke in the doctor's office he becomes aware of what really matters to him. Things that sixty seconds earlier had seemed all-important suddenly appear meaningless, while people and concerns that he had till then dismissed at once take on supreme importance.

Maybe, he realizes, working this weekend on that big deal at the office isn't all that vital. Maybe it's more important to fly cross-country for his grandson's graduation. Maybe it isn't so crucial that he have the last word in the fight with his wife. Maybe instead he should tell her how much she means to him and how deeply he has always loved her.

Other thoughts occur to the patient diagnosed as terminal. What about that gift he had for music? What became of the passion he once felt to work with the sick and the homeless? Why do these unlived lives return now with such power and poignancy?

Faced with our imminent extinction, Tom Laughlin believes, all assumptions are called into question. What does our life mean? Have we lived it right? Are there vital acts we've left unperformed, crucial words unspoken? Is it too late?

Tom Laughlin draws a diagram of the psyche, a Jungian-derived model that looks something like this:

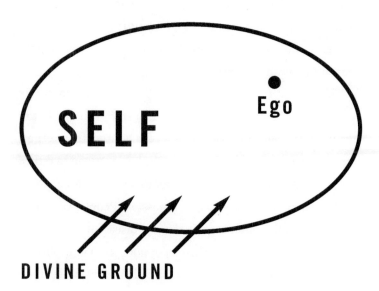

The Ego, Jung tells us, is that part of the psyche that we think of as "I." Our conscious intelligence. Our everyday brain that thinks, plans, and runs the show of our day-to-day life.

The Self, as Jung defined it, is a greater entity, which includes the Ego but also incorporates the Personal and Collective Unconscious. Dreams and intuitions come from the Self. The archetypes of the unconscious dwell there. It is, Jung believed, the sphere of the soul.

What happens in that instant when we learn we may soon die, Tom Laughlin contends, is that the seat of our consciousness shifts.

It moves from the Ego to the Self.

The world is entirely new, viewed from the Self. At once we discern what's really important. Superficial concerns fall away, replaced by a deeper, more profoundly grounded perspective.

This is how Tom Laughlin's foundation battles cancer. He counsels his clients not just to make that shift mentally but to live it out in their lives. He supports the housewife in resuming her career in social work, urges the businessman to return to the violin, assists the Vietnam vet to write his novel.

Miraculously, cancers go into remission. People recover. Is it possible, Tom Laughlin asks, that the disease itself evolved as a consequence of actions taken (or not taken) in our lives? Could our unlived lives have exacted their vengeance upon us in the form of cancer? And if they did, can we cure ourselves, now, by living these lives out?

THE EGO AND THE SELF

Here's what I think. I think angels make their home in the Self, while Resistance has its seat in the Ego.

The fight is between the two.

The Self wishes to create, to evolve. The Ego likes things just the way they are.

What is the Ego, anyway? Since this is my book, I'll define it my way.

The Ego is that part of the psyche that believes in material existence.

The Ego's job is to take care of business in the real world. It's an important job. We couldn't last a day without it. But there are worlds other than the real world, and this is where the Ego runs into trouble.

Here's what the Ego believes:

1) *Death is real.* The Ego believes that our existence is defined by our physical flesh. When the body dies, we die. There is no life beyond life.

2) *Time and space are real.* The Ego is analog. It believes that to get from A to Z we have to pass through B, C, and

D. To get from breakfast to supper we have to live the whole day.

3) *Every individual is different and separate from every other.* The Ego believes that I am distinct from you. The twain cannot meet. I can hurt you and it won't hurt me.

4) *The predominant impulse of life is self-preservation.* Because our existence is physical and thus vulnerable to innumerable evils, we live and act out of fear in all we do. It is wise, the Ego believes, to have children to carry on our line when we die, to achieve great things that will live after us, and to buckle our seat belts.

5) *There is no God.* No sphere exists except the physical and no rules apply except those of the material world.

These are the principles the Ego lives by. They are sound solid principles.

Here's what the Self believes:

1) *Death is an illusion.* The soul endures and evolves through infinite manifestations.

2) *Time and space are illusions.* Time and space operate only in the physical sphere, and even here, don't apply to dreams, visions, transports. In other dimensions we move "swift as thought" and inhabit multiple planes simultaneously.

3) *All beings are one.* If I hurt you, I hurt myself.

4) *The supreme emotion is love.* Union and mutual assistance are the imperatives of life. We are all in this together.

5) *God is all there is.* Everything that is, is God in one form or another. God, the divine ground, is that in which we live and move and have our being. Infinite planes of reality exist, all created by, sustained by and infused by the spirit of God.

EXPERIENCING THE SELF

Have you ever wondered why the slang terms for intoxication are so demolition-oriented? Stoned, smashed, hammered. It's because they're talking about the Ego. It's the Ego that gets blasted, waxed, plastered. We demolish the Ego to get to the Self.

The margins of the Self touch upon the Divine Ground. Meaning the Mystery, the Void, the source of Infinite Wisdom and Consciousness.

Dreams come from the Self. Ideas come from the Self. When we meditate we access the Self. When we fast, when we pray, when we go on a vision quest, it's the Self we're seeking. When the dervish whirls, when the yogi chants, when the sadhu mutilates his flesh; when penitents crawl a hundred miles on their knees, when Native Americans pierce themselves in the Sun Dance, when suburban kids take Ecstasy and dance all night at a rave, they're seeking the Self. When we deliberately alter our consciousness in any way, we're trying to find the Self. When the alcoholic collapses in the gutter, that voice that tells him, "I'll save you," comes from the Self.

The Self is our deepest being.

The Self is united to God.

The Self is incapable of falsehood.

The Self, like the Divine Ground that permeates it, is ever-growing and ever-evolving.

The Self speaks for the future.

That's why the Ego hates it.

The Ego hates the Self because when we seat our consciousness in the Self, we put the ego out of business.

The Ego doesn't want us to evolve. The Ego runs the show right now. It likes things just the way they are.

The instinct that pulls us toward art is the impulse to evolve, to learn, to heighten and elevate our consciousness. The Ego hates this. Because the more awake we become, the less we need the Ego.

The Ego hates it when the awakening writer sits down at the typewriter.

The Ego hates it when the aspiring painter steps up before the easel.

The Ego hates it because it knows that these souls are awakening to a call, and that that call comes from a plane nobler than the material one and from a source deeper and more powerful than the physical.

The Ego hates the prophet and the visionary because they propel the race upward. The Ego hated Socrates and Jesus, Luther and Galileo, Lincoln and JFK and Martin Luther King.

The Ego hates artists because they are the pathfinders and bearers of the future, because each one dares, in James Joyce's phrase, to "forge in the smithy of my soul the uncreated conscience of my race."

Such evolution is life-threatening to the Ego. It reacts accordingly. It summons its cunning, marshals its troops.

The Ego produces Resistance and attacks the awakening artist.

FEAR

Resistance feeds on fear. We experience Resistance as fear. But fear of what?

Fear of the consequences of following our heart. Fear of bankruptcy, fear of poverty, fear of insolvency. Fear of groveling when we try to make it on our own, and of groveling when we give up and come crawling back to where we started. Fear of being selfish, of being rotten wives or disloyal husbands; fear of failing to support our families, of sacrificing their dreams for ours. Fear of betraying our race, our 'hood, our homies. Fear of failure. Fear of being ridiculous. Fear of throwing away the education, the training, the preparation that those we love have sacrificed so much for, that we ourselves have worked our butts off for. Fear of launching into the void, of hurtling too far out there; fear of passing some point of no return, beyond which we cannot recant, cannot reverse, cannot rescind, but must live with this cocked-up choice for the rest of our lives. Fear of madness. Fear of insanity. Fear of death.

These are serious fears. But they're not the real fear. Not the Master Fear, the Mother of all Fears that's so close to us that even when we verbalize it we don't believe it.

Fear That We Will Succeed.

That we can access the powers we secretly know we possess.

That we can become the person we sense in our hearts we truly are.

This is the most terrifying prospect a human being can face, because it ejects him at one go (he imagines) from all the tribal inclusions his psyche is wired for and has been for fifty million years.

We fear discovering that we are more than we think we are. More than our parents/children/teachers think we are. We fear that we actually possess the talent that our still, small voice tells us. That we actually have the guts, the perseverance, the capacity. We fear that we truly can steer our ship, plant our flag, reach our Promised Land. We fear this because, if it's true, then we become estranged from all we know. We pass through a membrane. We become monsters and monstrous.

We know that if we embrace our ideals, we must prove worthy of them. And that scares the hell out of us. What will become of us? We will lose our friends and family, who will no longer recognize us. We will wind up alone, in the cold void of starry space, with nothing and no one to hold on to.

Of course this is exactly what happens. But here's the trick. We wind up in space, but not alone. Instead we are tapped into an unquenchable, undepletable, inexhaustible source of wisdom, consciousness, companionship. Yeah, we lose friends. But we find friends too, in places we never thought to look. And they're better friends, truer friends. And we're better and truer to them.

Do you believe me?

THE AUTHENTIC SELF

D o you have kids?

Then you know that not one of them popped out as *tabula rasa,* a blank slate. Each came into this world with a distinct and unique personality, an identity so set that you can fling stardust and great balls of fire at it and not morph it by one micro-dot. Each kid was who he was. Even identical twins, constituted of the exact same genetic material, were radically different from Day One and always would be.

Personally I'm with Wordsworth:

> Our birth is but a sleep and a forgetting:
> The soul that rises with us, our life's star,
> Hath had elsewhere its setting,
> And cometh from afar:
> Not in entire forgetfulness,
> And not in utter nakedness,
> But trailing clouds of glory do we come,
> From God who is our home.

In other words, none of us are born as passive generic

blobs waiting for the world to stamp its imprint on us. Instead we show up possessing already a highly refined and individuated soul.

Another way of thinking of it is this: We're not born with unlimited choices.

We can't be anything we want to be.

We come into this world with a specific, personal destiny. We have a job to do, a calling to enact, a self to become. We are who we are from the cradle, and we're stuck with it.

Our job in this lifetime is not to shape ourselves into some ideal we imagine we ought to be, but to find out who we already are and become it.

If we were born to paint, it's our job to become a painter.

If we were born to raise and nurture children, it's our job to become a mother.

If we were born to overthrow the order of ignorance and injustice of the world, it's our job to realize it and get down to business.

TERRITORY VERSUS HIERARCHY

I n the animal kingdom, individuals define themselves in one of two ways—by their rank within a hierarchy (a hen in a pecking order, a wolf in a pack) or by their connection to a territory (a home base, a hunting ground, a turf).

This is how individuals—humans as well as animals—achieve psychological security. They know where they stand. The world makes sense.

Of the two orientations, the hierarchical seems to be the default setting. It's the one that kicks in automatically when we're kids. We run naturally in packs and cliques; without thinking about it, we know who's the top dog and who's the underdog. And we know our own place. We define ourselves, instinctively it seems, by our position within the schoolyard, the gang, the club.

It's only later in life, usually after a stern education in the university of hard knocks, that we begin to explore the territorial alternative.

For some of us, this saves our lives.

THE HIERARCHICAL ORIENTATION

Most of us define ourselves hierarchically and don't even know it. It's hard not to. School, advertising, the entire materialist culture drills us from birth to define ourselves by others' opinions. Drink this beer, get this job, look this way and everyone will love you.

What is a hierarchy, anyway?

Hollywood is a hierarchy. So are Washington, Wall Street, and the Daughters of the American Revolution.

High school is the ultimate hierarchy. And it works; in a pond that small, the hierarchical orientation succeeds. The cheerleader knows where she fits, as does the dweeb in the Chess Club. Each has found a niche. The system works.

There's a problem with the hierarchical orientation, though. When the numbers get too big, the thing breaks down. A pecking order can hold only so many chickens. In Massapequa High, you can find your place. Move to Manhattan, and the trick no longer works. New York City is too big to function as a hierarchy. So is IBM. So is Michigan State. The individual in multitudes this vast feels overwhelmed, anonymous. He is submerged in the mass. He's lost.

We humans seem to have been wired by our evolutionary past to function most comfortably in a tribe of twenty to, say, eight hundred. We can push it maybe to a few thousand, even to five figures. But at some point it maxes out. Our brains can't file that many faces. We thrash around, flashing our badges of status (Hey, how do you like my Lincoln Navigator?) and wondering why nobody gives a shit.

We have entered Mass Society. The hierarchy is too big. It doesn't work anymore.

THE ARTIST AND THE HIERARCHY

For the artist to define himself hierarchically is fatal.

Let's examine why. First, let's look at what happens in a hierarchical orientation.

An individual who defines himself by his place in a pecking order will:

1) Compete against all others in the order, seeking to elevate his station by advancing against those above him, while defending his place against those beneath.

2) Evaluate his happiness/success/achievement by his rank within the hierarchy, feeling most satisfied when he's high and most miserable when he's low.

3) Act toward others based upon their rank in the hierarchy, to the exclusion of all other factors.

4) Evaluate his every move solely by the effect it produces on others. He will act for others, dress for others, speak for others, think for others.

But the artist cannot look to others to validate his efforts or his calling. If you don't believe me, ask Van Gogh, who produced masterpiece after masterpiece and never found a buyer in his whole life.

The artist must operate territorially. He must do his work for its own sake.

To labor in the arts for any reason other than love is prostitution. Recall the fate of Odysseus' men who slew the cattle of the sun.

> Their own witlessness cast them away.
> The fools! To destroy for meat the oxen
> of the most exalted Sun, wherefore the sun-god
> blotted out the day of their return.

In the hierarchy, the artist faces outward. Meeting someone new he asks himself, What can this person do for me? How can this person advance my standing?

In the hierarchy, the artist looks up and looks down. The one place he can't look is that place he must: within.

THE DEFINITION OF A HACK

I learned this from Robert McKee. A hack, he says, is a writer who second-guesses his audience. When the hack sits down to work, he doesn't ask himself what's in his own heart. He asks what the market is looking for.

The hack condescends to his audience. He thinks he's superior to them. The truth is, he's scared to death of them or, more accurately, scared of being authentic in front of them, scared of writing what he really feels or believes, what he himself thinks is interesting. He's afraid it won't sell. So he tries to anticipate what the market (a telling word) wants, then gives it to them.

In other words, the hack writes hierarchically. He writes what he imagines will play well in the eyes of others. He does not ask himself, What do I myself want to write? What do I think is important? Instead he asks, What's hot, what can I make a deal for?

The hack is like the politician who consults the polls before he takes a position. He's a demagogue. He panders.

It can pay off, being a hack. Given the depraved state of American culture, a slick dude can make millions being a hack. But even if you succeed, you lose, because you've

152 | THE WAR OF ART

sold out your Muse, and your Muse is you, the best part of yourself, where your finest and only true work comes from.

I was starving as a screenwriter when the idea for *The Legend of Bagger Vance* came to me. It came as a book, not a movie. I met with my agent to give him the bad news. We both knew that first novels take forever and sell for nothing. Worse, a novel about golf, even if we could find a publisher, is a straight shot to the remainder bin.

But the Muse had me. I had to do it. To my amazement, the book succeeded critically and commercially better than anything I'd ever done, and others since have been lucky too. Why? My best guess is this: I trusted what I wanted, not what I thought would work. I did what I myself thought was interesting, and left its reception to the gods.

The artist can't do his work hierarchically. He has to work territorially.

THE TERRITORIAL ORIENTATION

There's a three-legged coyote who lives up the hill from me. All the garbage cans in the neighborhood belong to him. It's his territory. Every now and then some four-legged intruder tries to take over. They can't do it. On his home turf, even a peg-leg critter is invincible.

We humans have territories too. Ours are psychological. Stevie Wonder's territory is the piano. Arnold Schwarzenegger's is the gym. When Bill Gates pulls into the parking lot at Microsoft, he's on his territory. When I sit down to write, I'm on mine.

What are the qualities of a territory?

1) *A territory provides sustenance.* Runners know what a territory is. So do rock climbers and kayakers and yogis. Artists and entrepreneurs know what a territory is. The swimmer who towels off after finishing her laps feels a helluva lot better than the tired, cranky person who dove into the pool thirty minutes earlier.

2) *A territory sustains us without any external input.* A territory is a closed feedback loop. Our role is to put in

effort and love; the territory absorbs this and gives it back to us in the form of well-being.

When experts tell us that exercise (or any other effort-requiring activity) banishes depression, this is what they mean.

3) *A territory can only be claimed alone.* You can team with a partner, you can work out with a friend, but you only need yourself to soak up your territory's juice.

4) *A territory can only be claimed by work.* When Arnold Schwarzenegger hits the gym, he's on his own turf. But what made it his own are the hours and years of sweat he put in to claim it. A territory doesn't give, it gives back.

5) *A territory returns exactly what you put in.* Territories are fair. Every erg of energy you put in goes infallibly into your account. A territory never devalues. A territory never crashes. What you deposited, you get back, dollar-for-dollar.

What's your territory?

THE ARTIST AND THE TERRITORY

The act of creation is by definition territorial. As the mother-to-be bears her child within her, so the artist or innovator contains her new life. No one can help her give it birth. But neither does she need any help.

The mother and the artist are watched over by heaven. Nature's wisdom knows when it's time for the life within to switch from gills to lungs. It knows down to the nanosecond when the first tiny fingernails may appear.

When the artist acts hierarchically, she short-circuits the Muse. She insults her and pisses her off.

The artist and the mother are vehicles, not originators. They don't create the new life, they only bear it. This is why birth is such a humbling experience. The new mom weeps in awe at the little miracle in her arms. She knows it came out of her but not from her, through her but not of her.

When the artist works territorially, she reveres heaven. She aligns herself with the mysterious forces that power the universe and that seek, through her, to bring forth new life. By doing her work for its own sake, she sets herself at the service of these forces.

Remember, as artists we don't know diddly. We're

winging it every day. For us to try to second-guess our Muse the way a hack second-guesses his audience is condescension to heaven. It's blasphemy and sacrilege.

Instead let's ask ourselves like that new mother: What do I feel growing inside me? Let me bring that forth, if I can, for its own sake and not for what it can do for me or how it can advance my standing.

THE DIFFERENCE BETWEEN
TERRITORY AND HIERARCHY

How can we tell if our orientation is territorial or hierarchical?

One way is to ask ourselves, If I were feeling really anxious, what would I do? If we would pick up the phone and call six friends, one after the other, with the aim of hearing their voices and reassuring ourselves that they still love us, we're operating hierarchically.

We're seeking the good opinion of others.

What would Arnold Schwarzenegger do on a freaky day? He wouldn't phone his buddies; he'd head for the gym. He wouldn't care if the place was empty, if he didn't say a word to a soul. He knows that working out, all by itself, is enough to bring him back to his center.

His orientation is territorial.

Here's another test. Of any activity you do, ask yourself: If I were the last person on earth, would I still do it?

If you're all alone on the planet, a hierarchical orientation makes no sense. There's no one to impress. So, if you'd still pursue that activity, congratulations. You're doing it territorially.

If Arnold Schwarzenegger were the last man on earth,

he'd still go the gym. Stevie Wonder would still pound the piano. The sustenance they get comes from the act itself, not from the impression it makes on others. I have a friend who's nuts for clothes. If she were the last woman on earth, she would shoot straight to Givenchy or St. Laurent, smash her way in, and start pillaging. In her case, it wouldn't be to impress others. She just loves clothes. That's her territory.

Now: What about ourselves as artists?

How do we do our work? Hierarchically or territorially?

If we were freaked out, would we go there first?

If we were the last person on earth, would we still show up at the studio, the rehearsal hall, the laboratory?

THE SUPREME VIRTUE

Someone once asked the Spartan king Leonidas to identify the supreme warrior virtue from which all others flowed. He replied: "Contempt for death."

For us as artists, read "failure." Contempt for failure is our cardinal virtue. By confining our attention territorially to our own thoughts and actions—in other words, to the work and its demands—we cut the earth from beneath the blue-painted, shield-banging, spear-brandishing foe.

THE FRUITS OF OUR LABOR

When Krishna instructed Arjuna that we have a right to our labor but not to the fruits of our labor, he was counseling the warrior to act territorially, not hierarchically. We must do our work for its own sake, not for fortune or attention or applause.

Then there's the third way proffered by the Lord of Discipline, which is beyond both hierarchy and territory. That is to do the work and give it to Him. Do it as an offering to God.

> Give the act to me.
> Purged of hope and ego,
> Fix your attention on the soul.
> Act and do for me.

The work comes from heaven anyway. Why not give it back?

To labor in this way, *The Bhagavad-Gita* tells us, is a form of meditation and a supreme species of spiritual devotion. It also, I believe, conforms most closely to Higher Reality. In fact, we are servants of the Mystery. We were put here on earth to act as agents of the Infinite, to bring into existence that which is not yet, but which will be, through us.

Every breath we take, every heartbeat, every evolution of every cell comes from God and is sustained by God every second, just as every creation, invention, every bar of music or line of verse, every thought, vision, fantasy, every dumb-ass flop and stroke of genius comes from that infinite intelligence that created us and the universe in all its dimensions, out of the Void, the field of infinite potential, primal chaos, the Muse. To acknowledge that reality, to efface all ego, to let the work come through us and give it back freely to its source, that, in my opinion, is as true to reality as it gets.

PORTRAIT OF THE ARTIST

In the end, we arrive at a kind of model of the artist's world, and that model is that there exist other, higher planes of reality, about which we can prove nothing, but from which arise our lives, our work, and our art. These spheres are trying to communicate with ours. When Blake said Eternity is in love with the creations of time, he was referring to those planes of pure potential, which are timeless, placeless, spaceless, but which long to bring their visions into being here, in this timebound, space-defined world.

The artist is the servant of that intention, those angels, that Muse. The enemy of the artist is the small-time Ego, which begets Resistance, which is the dragon that guards the gold. That's why an artist must be a warrior and, like all warriors, artists over time acquire modesty and humility. They may, some of them, conduct themselves flamboyantly in public. But alone with the work they are chaste and humble. They know they are not the source of the creations they bring into being. They only facilitate. They carry. They are the willing and skilled instruments of the gods and goddesses they serve.

THE ARTIST'S LIFE

A re you a born writer? Were you put on earth to be a painter, a scientist, an apostle of peace? In the end the question can only be answered by action.

Do it or don't do it.

It may help to think of it this way. If you were meant to cure cancer or write a symphony or crack cold fusion and you don't do it, you not only hurt yourself, even destroy yourself. You hurt your children. You hurt me. You hurt the planet.

You shame the angels who watch over you and you spite the Almighty, who created you and only you with your unique gifts, for the sole purpose of nudging the human race one millimeter farther along its path back to God.

Creative work is not a selfish act or a bid for attention on the part of the actor. It's a gift to the world and every being in it. Don't cheat us of your contribution. Give us what you've got.

WITH GRATITUDE

For their generous permission to quote from their works,
the author acknowledges the following sources:

STEVEN PRESSFIELD is the author of *Gates of Fire, Tides of War, The Afghan Campaign, The Profession, The Warrior Ethos* and *Turning Pro,* among others. He is a former Marine. In 2003, he was made an honorary citizen by the city of Sparta in Greece.